GIVING
CHARITIES GREEN

A Funded & Practical Guide to Taking Your Charity Green

ALEX VERSLUIS, P.Eng., P.E., C.E.M.

Published in Toronto, Canada

Print ISBN: 978-0-9950414-0-0

Ebook ISBN: 978-0-9950414-1-7

For my wife...who completes me! You discovered me in 1991 at McGill University in Montreal as a fun-loving, ambitious, and clueless "Granola". You inspire me, motivate me, support me, love me and are the best editor for which a husband could hope!

For my two beautiful boys, Jeffrey and Matthew, who are the reason I wrote this book. We have brought you into a world full of potential and opportunity, but you and your fellow Millennials will suffer the impacts from generations of over-consumption and greed. I know you will find and make the tools to break this wave and chart a new course. You will be the recovery generation.

A special thanks to my big brother, Rolf Versluis. Not only is he one of the smartest people I know, but he is also an exceptional editor, an amazing dad and husband, and the IT guy to IT guys.

"We make a living by what we get, but we make a life by what we give."
  - Winston Churchill

PROLOGUE

I was exhilarated – but now had that feeling of adrenaline draining from my bloodstream after giving a high-energy presentation to a room full of corporate executives with an appetite for "green." It was the summer of 2013, and I had just left the stage having presented our approach to building green spaces at the YMCA of Greater Toronto with the help of the communities who volunteer and donate money to breathe new life into these energy-efficient and beautiful spaces for those communities to enjoy. Mathis, an exceptional ecologist who had helped to facilitate the design for all of the Y's green roofs, had presented an interactive 3D computer model for the 60,000 square-foot green roof for our new YMCA building that would first be used as part of the 2015 Pan Am Games in Toronto – and the session was electric with audience participation. We even had questions about how we managed to sell our carbon offsets from our energy-savings work on other YMCAs across our GTA region.

Being an introverted person, I found a quiet place to collect my thoughts and marvel at how I had the opportunity to talk about our exciting projects at this conference and get the word out that other charities can do this too. I was approached by an unassuming young man who was beaming from the presentation, and he proceeded to share the following incredible opportunity with me. "I can't believe the timing!" he said. "We just learned this week that we won a huge grant, and we now just need a partner – and the Y is perfect!"

He was part of a company that had been awarded a grant for $10 million to try out a new electric vehicle charging station and battery system controlled by his cutting edge technology. It was funded through the local power authority and our provincial government and they had everything they needed; except, a partner to house the equipment.

The YMCA fit the bill – we are a public-facing charity with significant real estate, and our mission is to improve the health of the communities in a way that is transparent, relies on partners and is done in an environmentally sustainable way – it was exactly what the YMCA of Greater Toronto was seeking. In brief, they would like to place $1 million of equipment that would save on electricity costs, allow us to provide electric vehicle charging stations in our parking lot and a solar photo voltaic (PV) panel on the roof of our building as long as we would let them use, study and share the results. It was a perfect match.

I'd been getting at least two calls a month for these types of potential partnerships, and many have worked out. Sometimes it has been a municipality that wanted to partner on a project, a corporation that wanted to place volunteers with us and had money to support their work. This is what it looks like on the other side.

As Col. Smith from the A-Team always says: "I love it when a plan comes together!"

Table of Contents

INTRODUCTION

TAKING YOUR CHARITY GREEN...FOR REAL

You are ready to make a change. You know there is a better way, you just don't know how. You are a charity, you have no "extra" money, no expertise, no time – but people keep asking, keep offering ideas, keep offering to help. It feels like you are walking down a dark corridor with little bursts of light on one idea or another...but how does it fit together? Everything is about businesses, how does this affect a charity? What is the first step, and where are we going? You picked up this book because it not only says it will help to explain this, but to actually improve your fundraising efforts...pinch me, right?

I have wrestled with these questions. I spent a lot of the first part of my career in the private sector, in both the US and Canada, working in, managing and running businesses. I am an engineer, so I need to build a system, develop and evolve it, then test it. I am a father, and want my sons' generation to enjoy this planet. I am a philanthropist at heart, so I want to share this system for others to use. Having spent a lot of time volunteering for charities as a child and adult, and now in my seventh year working for the YMCA in Toronto, Canada, I get it. I started down that dark hallway, didn't know what door to open, which person to trust or where to start. This is my perspective, my system (with a lot of help from a lot of people) and what worked for me, interlaced with my life stories that offer some context and motivation. The results have exceeded my expectations and have stumbled onto something that is actually rather spectacular. I hope you agree.

ILLUMINATION

Why is it that businesses who manufacture, sell, maintain and even many that consult on green want you to think going green means spending a lot of money on green technology or high efficiency energy-consuming equipment? Sadly, this only moves the needle a small amount, and the money you need is locked up in your inefficient buildings. Technology is a piece of the plan, but only one of the many tools, and often falls flat after the investments are made. The two most significant activities for taking your organization green are to *Change How You Think* and to *Affect Real Behavioral Change*. Once you instill order and direction, the ripple effect within your organization is exponential and unstoppable. And when you extend this ripple outside your organization and into the individuals and businesses in the community, it has the power to drive real change.

Have you ever sat at a traffic light with no power and marveled at the inefficiency and chaos a simple traffic light can prevent at a busy intersection? I have pondered this, usually in a symphony of honking horns with a chorus of expletives from adjacent vehicles, and marveled how three light bulbs and some basic logic can create so much efficiency of time. But as you look deeper, it is more than the colorful box that creates this efficiency. We have reasonable trust that the lights will be red in the opposite direction when ours is green and we have established some behavior patterns in the form of rules.

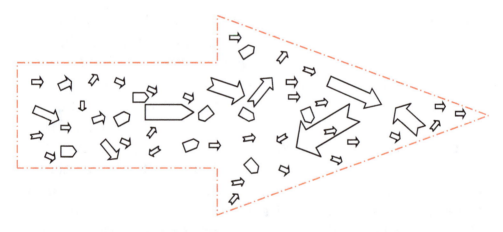

Just like the cars on the road, most of the organizations that I have been exposed to have many people heading in different directions with different information and goals. Often the goals are aligned, but different, and the information is partial. A passionate leader, executive support, and a smart plan with clear principles will be your traffic light to start moving your organization in the same direction…and turn that light green!

Oh, and you may drive significant funding to your charity doing in the process...Bring On The Green!

What is the real goal of the environmental movement? For me, it is to return the planet to a point where it can heal itself - where it can be sustaining and reverse the negative accumulated impacts to a point where we as a race can continue to live on this planet and future generations can enjoy its rich biodiversity as we have - no less, no more.

What does that look like? Strip down all the lingo, sexy technology, rhetoric from both extremes and you have a simple solution - **drive behavioral change**. We need to work toward an enlightened culture where people think about the impact of their choices and embed sustainability at an atomic level. As Aristotle says "We are what we do repeatedly." Help people make a new choice by showing them the way, explaining the repercussions, and having them repeat the choice at least 5 times. It's parenting 101.

Why are charities and Not-For-Profits (NFPs) well positioned to drive this type of change? We are already working with all segments of the population to achieve our respective missions. By using this additional cause as a means to achieve our mission, we will be doing our jobs better and in a way that leaves a healthier planet for future generations. As charities, we bring communities together, raise awareness, educate, motivate, and we usually do it in a rational and positive way.

In the US, there are more than 1.5 million active charities employing more than 13.5 million people that make up 10% of the workforce and they are in every community – more than the entire finance sector, including insurance and real estate combined. In Canada, there are close to 90,000 charities employing more than 2 million people – more than the mining, oil and gas industry combined (references http://www.independentsector.org/economic_role) that's a lot of people, not even counting all of those people who volunteer and support all of these charities.

In the future, I envision charities as one of the critical weaves in the fabric that will bind the ultimate solution of collective behavioral change. In that environment, anything and everything is possible. As charities, we are on the ground, embedded in our communities, and we interact with all walks of life. We are trusted, credible, and seek to improve the world without ulterior motives.

The starting point begins by helping the staff within your charity or NFP understand the goal, and how to get there. This will motivate action!

Next, you invite volunteers and donors to participate in Green Teams to improve how the charity is operating, while learning, teaching and demonstrating successes. You know you are heading in the right direction when your Green Teams connect outside your walls and into the communities. They will start to partner with: corporations, government groups, local residents, universities and other educational institutions. They will start to band together and transfer that knowledge into everyone's homes, businesses, green spaces – deep into the communities helping to create community Green Teams.

As these diverse groups connect, that fabric is woven using the loom of your design. This is your time to add your charity's threads to the community fabric.

How can businesses and governments help to drive this change?
Some already are - it is about taking Corporate Social Responsibility (CSR) teams to the next level! Businesses and government groups often see themselves as funders; and yes, this is one of the necessary ingredients of making this work. The other ingredient is people. By adding their staff, they add the other critical element to drive change. Funding often starts the reaction, but staff teams become the catalyst that amplifies the effect. This book describes a model that relies on businesses to participate with charities to form both the warp and the weave of the community fabric.

Businesses that have a genuine social conscience are starting to realize the impact this has on their staff. Current generations are taking less pay, working more productively, taking fewer sick days and are genuinely happier when their company enhances their community socially while being environmental sustainable.

We all have that need to see our work create some positive impact on society, some more than others. It's that hole in the chest that feels like "what's the point of this? I love what I do, it pays the bills,

but to what end?" Corporations that engage in their communities help to fill that hole and keep their staff happy. Happy staff means more productive staff, which yields greater production. If they are smart about it, they structure their brand to be aligned with community impact and build positive marketing opportunities to ensure their community recognizes their impact. Don't take my
word for it, look at your own buying habits.

While this book is geared towards empowering charities with the tools to create the capacity for this work to happen, businesses and individuals are the other hand in the "handshake"...else, we are just flapping our hands about. The approach described through this book is working with numerous businesses achieving their CSR goals....this book gives you a window into what to look for when placing your donations and staff time.

What motivates me? When I seek advice from someone, I love to absorb their stories and perspectives. But, I also need to understand their biases and what drives them. It only seems fair that I disclose my motivations:

To ensure each child reaches their potential; is offered opportunities to explore and learn; is given hope; is supported; and, their creativity is nurtured and encouraged to bloom so they can offer their gift to give. I want them to experience the things that inspired me and have opportunities to find new ones. I want them to learn and appreciate the outdoors - hike, camp, canoe, kayak, sail, rock climb, and see nature in its pure unadulterated form. I want my kids' great-grandkids to be able to know a vibrant and diverse forest, to enjoy clean waterways, and to breathe fresh air.

My goal is to help swing the pendulum back to a more neutral position, giving the planet a chance to heal and exist for kids to explore. I want to make sure they learn how to heal the planet, and to keep the planet healthy. *I want to see these effects in my lifetime.*

If you speak with a child, they know in their little hearts that all life should be valued, from bugs to animals – new sprouts to 500 year old redwoods. We just need to stop getting in their way, give them the tools and knowledge to let them help us correct course and watch how their innovation and creativity works its magic – I believe this to the depths of my soul.

As you see the themes emerging throughout this book, you will see it is not just about *doing* the "right thing", it is about doing it in a way that a lot of people can participate and are educated through the process. You will be surprised at how it also builds community and brings people together...and yes, it gets funded...really!

You will learn my Magic Formula

This book outlines the formula I helped to develop, taking a prominent charity from wanting to do the right thing for the environment, to having national recognition as one of the top community charities for being green – a journey that has no end, but clear direction. OK, it is not magic; instead, it is a process that requires passionate people, the ability to mobilize change, compassion for life and courage to take a step. This is the guidebook that can be a helpful tool along your journey and I will be your tour guide using my experience to point you in a direction that worked for me. The website, www.GivingCharitiesGreen.com has been created to offer some continuity to this process and to add depth and breadth to this adventure. Check it out and join the discussion.

The Goal: To use charities as a meeting place. A place where anyone and everyone can come together to share their time, their business products, their money and their ideas in a non-political, non-corporate, safe, and credible way where there are no competitions, just a good cause working with the community to drive the change to heal our planet.

First step: Get charities to become sustainable themselves and to understand their impact. This is part one of this book, "Look Before You Leap."

Second step: Have charities create and facilitate projects, initiatives and events that drive behavioral change through community-engaged projects that educate and bring people together. This is part 2 of this book, "Action."

Last step: People who have learned and participated, start to do this at home, in their businesses or workplaces, and the tidal wave grows. This just happens.

I believe every organization – especially NFPs and charities – are already doing some great environmental initiatives and are already a bit "green". The fun part of moving your organization to a deeper shade of green is to learn and discover, then bind these groups of people together, collect these initiatives and coordinate this into a plan that takes your charity down the path as an organized team. Doing it in a way that brings in more donations, greater resources, and high-level volunteers...well, that is just cool.

What this book is not:

This book is designed to help you move into action, following the not-so "magic formula". What this book does not cover is why all this is important. There are some incredibly smart, highly visible and well-connected people who are doing this really well. They are talking about the impending ecological disaster that is our planet, how humanity has become a force of nature by over-consuming, over-polluting, over-populating. Now the effects are being manifested in real climatic change that will affect the lifestyle of current generations. It is not "if", it is how bad and how soon.

I would recommend that you educate yourself on current research, read the reports created by the Intergovernmental Panel on Climatic Change (IPCC), watch Al Gore's "An Inconvenient Truth" or his more recent "An Option," look through David Suzuki's Foundation website, watch some of the YouTube videos "The Most Terrifying Video You'll Ever See" and "The Most Important Video You will ever see" (all 8 parts) to name some oldies but goodies. More is generated daily, but the message is clear:

Humans have taken too much from the planet and we need to act more responsibly, to repair the damage to the planet, protect the remaining rich biodiversity – like the threads of a surgeon to stop the bleeding – and to help it heal. Each of us has a role the play.

 Twitter Moment:

As you read this book, I would love your opinion...a poll that breaks all the rules of pollsters. I don't care about statistical relevance, age, sex, gender...I just want to know if I'm on-track as it compares to your experience. As I present concepts, I will give you choices to tweet or ask for your opinions and examples. It is an experiment that will demonstrate who is reading and how people feel. I will show the results on our website, GivingCharitiesGreen.com Try it now, after reading that section, are you inspired to make a change...did I get it right? I can see you looking at your PDA or computer, give it whirl! Consider this one of your green acts of the day. Feel free to tweet whenever you get goosebumps or disagree. Your involvement will only make this process better!

Include @GivingGreen and one of the following comments.

>   "I am inspired" or "not inspired"

Example: @GivingGreen **I am inspired** by your intro...I believe!

Example: @GivingGreen You are delirious, totally **not inspired**...I'm giving this book to charity!

Not on Twitter? This is a great way to start and try it, it is free and takes 10 minutes to setup...then you can join the discussion in a way that helps to improve our planet. Go to www.twitter.com (or ask anyone between the ages of 11 and 31) and make a meaningful contribution to this virtual world.

It is not the strongest of the species that survive, nor the most intelligent, but the one most responsive to change.
  - Charles Darwin

If it ain't broke, don't fix it.
  - Popularized by Bert Lance

Chapter 1 - The Giving Charities Green Concept ...and Why This Works

Charities and Not-For-Profits (NFPs) have a unique struggle to balance mission with dollars raised. When adding anything new to the already overflowing plate, it stresses this balance, and it is too easy to dismiss as "off-mission". All charities have a mission – its reason for doing what it does, to make some positive contribution to their community – that must remain the core focus. There is also the struggle with the fact that this mission needs money, dollars, time, support...and that relies on asking all types of people for time, treasure and talent. Many charities have lagged in helping their organizations *go green* because they perceive this as a "distracting initiative" that will take the focus off the mission. They just don't understand the impact, and the unknown amount of work and the "distraction" is too daunting.

What I have found is that the inverse is actually true. People who work for and with charities have a huge appetite for making the sustainable choice. They are already believers – many doing it in their own personal lives. They have hearts of gold and need no convincing. For some commercial organizations, that has been one of the barriers of success, getting employee buy-in, but even this is starting to change. The real challenge is to get the attention of senior management; to make the case that *going green* will actually enhance your core mission by demonstrating you are current, competent, and appreciate how your organization fits into the world at large. As well, **it will actually drive money and volunteers** to your organization.

My proposal is to do more of the same, just with an eye to green. Don't change what works, enhance and integrate into your already successful organization. Develop a **"Giving-Green Fund"** or **"Green Fund"** – a fund to accept gifts to your organization with a focus on the green initiatives that is part of your charity's donor-centered giving strategy.

This provides a specific fund that you can use to reduce your energy consumption and start to implement other initiatives as you develop your organization's approach to environmental sustainability.

For many organizations, traditional giving is directed to operational needs, to capital projects, or to an endowment fund – but many of those operational and capital projects are not "sexy" or easy to have organizations to fund. While the endowment allows charities to use the interest earned and keep the principal for future years and is a gift that keeps giving. This "Green Fund" concept flips the endowment approach on its head and works as follows:

Your charity builds a suite of projects and initiatives that will meet your key environmental goals. People who give money to this will be helping to fund projects that will create annual operational savings immediately. The operational savings are captured and redirected to assist your existing programming AND will help you reach your environmental goals. You provide feedback on progress and completion to steward your donors. You build your projects in a way that maximizes volunteer involvement.

What does the donor get?

They meet their philanthropic goals to donate money and time towards a project or fund in a charity they believe in.

+

They are improving the health of the environment in their own community or near the areas they operate (sometimes a primary goal.)

+

The savings from their gift continue to fund the charity year after year.

For example: Let's say instead of donating $25,000 to your endowment, that a corporate or individual donor places their money in your "Green Fund" toward a $25,000 project to replace the old lights in your building. Instead of the $2,000 in interest that you hope to make each year, the following happens: you save $9,000 of operational expenses **per year.** If you contact your local municipality first, you can probably get a $2,500 to $4,000 grant as well – that goes right to the bottom line. On top of this, you reduce the environmental impact by 10 tonnes of CO_2 per year – what a great story! Voila! (I have a plethora of examples in Part II: Action.)

Financially, you are making the equivalent of a return on your investment of 40% in lieu of the 8%, you have lowered your environmental impact, your donor feels great for not only helping your organization do the great work that you do, but improve the environmental impact to your community. Plus, you have new lights…that don't flicker!

This is a conservative example, doesn't include the power of volunteering, and I don't even mention the fact that you might later sell your carbon credits for more money – but I am getting ahead of myself. See the next example later in this chapter that shows the other end of the spectrum with donations, publicity and full volunteer engagement.

But…my lights are working just fine and I need money for doing the real charity work!

This is your chance to pause and think about all the inefficiencies in your operations to work better, smarter and with less waste – financially and environmentally. Your buildings are running on technology made first commercially feasible by Thomas Edison – a brilliant man, but his ideas are more than 130 years old…seriously. There is more computing power in your iPhone than NASA had in 1969, and they got a man to the moon! Trust me, you need new lights, and that is just the beginning. What is also missing are a segment of donors who already know this – believe this – and want to help reduce wasted energy in their communities. You need to position your organization to be able to ask for that help and receive it. Now is your time.

But...why would people and corporations donate to us? We are just starting to get our act together.

Great question! This book gives you the roadmap to define your organization's opportunities to dovetail your charity's mission - votre raison d'être - with the many points of synergy that exist to move our planet back to being healthy. You will build your charity's credibility of striving to be Sustainably Green by defining your vision, establishing your principles, creating your implementation strategy, then leading change, finding the resources and getting the word out. It is a recipe for success - you just need to start cooking!

Are you ready to lead change?

Take some time with this question. I believe the most important part of a successful transition to moving your organization to a deeper shade of green is a passionate person. This might be you. You should seriously think about it being you; however, this doesn't have to be you – you can still find that person in your organization, support that person and build that confidence while playing a role in this journey. Still, if you think you might be able to do it, you can be the one. You need to be willing and able to demand change. You need to build support, you need to build a plan, and you need to push until you see change. Once it starts, it is an amazing ride!

Ask yourself: Is this important to me? Am I organized? What is stopping me?

But..."*my manager doesn't understand being sustainable" or "we looked at that and we just don't have the time.*" Do your research. I spent my "volunteer" hours doing research, learning what had been done, what worked, what failed, who had tried and given up, who was doing it in their own little way. I built an inventory of what was already being done and it boggled my mind. This book is based on the results of all that work, and if it worked for me, it should work for you.

But..."*we don't have the money to do this.*" I have met with many people over the last few years and discussed the "Green Fund" concept and EVERY SINGLE PERSON WAS AMAZED!! This is your ace in the hole. Take this message to heart, develop examples that will be obvious next steps or small wins for your organization and make it happen. This is your chance to help make the difference and bring funding to your charity.

But..."*we don't have the people power to do the work that is required. It will take too much money to hire those resources.*" There is a phenomenal amount of free help that will be at your beck and call once you have support from the leadership. I had two interns that were paid for by the federal government who helped me put together the background information, apply for grants, start Green Teams, and start to drive change. Since those internships expired, I was able to build a simple business case (see www.GivingCharitiesGreen.com/staff_business_case) to explain why this person should be on staff full time. As well, we have endless volunteers from all backgrounds and experience levels helping us. We recently developed a team of volunteer interns staffed by recent Environmental Sciences graduates who couldn't find work in their chosen industry. As they worked as a waiter, barista, retailer, etc., they offered 10 to 25 hours per week to help our cause. While I couldn't pay them money, I could offer them something concrete on their resume and a reference to prospective employers. This resume building support has transitioned many of our volunteers to full-time roles in the sustainability sector. This is collaboration at its best!

But..."you worked for a big charity with resources. We are small."

As they say, it is not the size of the dog in the fight, but the fight in the dog. What I didn't have was a little book that told me what to do. You do. It isn't perfect, but it gives you principles that you can use to suit your organization, it gives you a plan that has worked for me and can be altered to suit your circumstances, and it gives you confidence that it can be done and should be done. The YMCA is a charity (in case you don't know) that surrounds the globe. The YMCA of Greater Toronto is one of the largest Ys in the world and I proved this works. Anything can be simplified down, but not everything can be amplified up. Use this book and the website as a guide, no matter your size. It will work. Stop making excuses.

Are you a Volunteer or Donor to a charity that wants to help instill this culture of sustainability?

Great! You don't have to work at a charity to have impact. You can be this champion or work with a staff member to drive change. Support is needed in all sectors of charities. There is not only one solution - just passionate people getting organized and getting the conversation started in a way that will get the right people talking. To be successful, this has to be a partnership with internal staff and external volunteers and donors. Put together the right people and you're off to the races!

Example of a project that achieves this not-so "magic formula" that includes full community engagement...and we did it within the first year of our conscious decision to "go green".

When you think of the YMCA, many think of basketball courts and pools. At our largest Health & Fitness Centre in our 25-year old Central Toronto YMCA building. This building had a massive roof - the size of 4 basketball courts - that was leaking. It had an outdoor running track and was used (rarely) by runners and sun bathers who worked up an amazing sweat in the suffocating heat. A concrete wasteland set in the middle of downtown Toronto. We took a risk – we knew that this space was poorly used, it needed a massive amount of work to fix and to prevent our gymnasium from going under water, but we saw this as an opportunity. The building is almost encircled with condos who stare out their windows at our 10,000 square foot space. It screamed for a facelift, but how? And how much?

After some internal discussions, we decided we would remove the concrete surface, replace the roof membrane and put back an intensive green roof in lieu of the concrete. This was a decision that required us to budget for an extra $200,000 in funding that we would seek through grants, individual and corporate donations. This was a risk, one that

would put us on the map if we did it well by creating the largest publicly accessible green roof in the City of Toronto, and demonstrate to the public our commitment to working in partnership to seek

healthy communities that include the health of our environment. We selected an incredible green roof consultant that helped us through all stages of the process. Yes, some sleep was lost.

The second risk that we decided to take was to reach into the community and connect to local residents, members of the gym and childcare, local business owners, local politicians, and asked their opinion on how we should design this space. This method, called by some Participatory Design, is a process that engages the user in all aspects of the design process to ensure the space will ultimately meet their needs, not those of a few well-placed executives. It can be successful if managed well, but can blow up if done poorly. Fortunately, we did it well.

We created a voluntary Green Roof Steering Committee that included a combination of current members, local business owners and local residents. They worked with our staff and defined the base requirements to ensure we would build a safe space. They also defined the structural limitations, occupancy standards and base principles like maximizing participant usage by remaining flexible with low maintenance. We established principles such as: all plantings would be local species that would further encourage local insects and birds to use the space to enhance biodiversity. We would restrict people from eating and drinking in the space. We would maximize the amount of recycled content (virtually 100%) and the space would be fully accessible to persons with disabilities. Educational signage would be developed to educate users on the green roof features and how it was constructed. We would also strive to add additional alternative energy technology to create more opportunities for education.

The fun began with our engagement campaign where we used many forms of communication to interact with our community to seek their feedback, in a way that would be convenient and maximize participation. We posted a blog, we sent emails, we set up in the lobby at different times of day, and we convened town hall meetings to seek opinions. Most of this work was done by willing and enthusiastic volunteers, supported by YMCA staff. We started by asking: "What would you want to see in this space?" We received a lot of responses for typical green roof concepts like: a water fountain, plants, benches, a place to stretch and work out. Also some bigger ideas like: a tennis court, fitness studio, and, my personal favorite, a driving range for golfers!

We narrowed the field and presented three designs that incorporated many different ideas, then requested feedback. We received the feedback in a way that allowed us to highlight the items people liked and disliked from each design (trying to avoid one design versus the other.) Throughout this engagement process, we created educational pieces that we would leave in public areas that described different finishes, plantings, lighting, water features, etc. In the end, we presented a final design that considered all the feedback, maintained our base principles and was a space to be proud of. The final design kept the running track along the perimeter for walking and running, and we created a 1,800 square-foot multi-use space for yoga and other group fitness classes, meetings, and events.

Then it was time to build it! We created a work plan that included contractors and volunteer work groups to carry the incredible momentum of interest and passion that was stirred throughout this process. We established shifts, defined the extent of work, built in safety training, and started to sign people and businesses up. We ended up turning people away as we wanted to keep the numbers to a manageable size, to ensure we had quality workmanship and happy volunteers. All ages participated, especially on the days we planted. The fabric of our volunteers included all skill levels, backgrounds, abilities, ages, religions and shape.

Some of the most successful synergies that formed were ones that we never planned, like an architectural student from a local university who I asked to project manage the volunteer schedule in partnership with some of the staff - she was later offered a job from an architect who also volunteered. One of the volunteers that helped throughout the construction ended up chairing our Green Team; six months later, he won a federally-funded internship position at the YMCA to help write sustainability policies that are currently in-use.

The media response was overwhelming. Local television stations interviewed us, Canadian Broadcast Corporation (CBC) did a radio segment and tons of newspaper and online media interviewed us for articles and recorded our progress. We were courted by many companies to get involved in a sponsorship role. In the end, TD Securities made a $250,000 donation to this project, believing in our mission and applauding our approach. RONA also made a gift-in-kind for much of the recycled plastic decking materials (TREX decking), and Ainsworth donated the design and installation of a demonstration-sized solar photovoltaic panel that connected into the electrical system and runs the LED lighting and the water fountain pumps. The City of Toronto's Eco-Roof program invested $24,300 based on the amount of wastewater they forecasted we would reduce once the roof was completed.

We had over 2,500 people in the community get involved during the design period, and over 150 volunteers give more than 1,500 volunteer hours to construct the space. Today, the roof is maintained by volunteers who use this to host a green speakers' series, an annual eco-fair, movie nights under stars, and weekly gardening and many other events as well.

This project shows what is possible when you use the approach described in this book. It allowed an organization that was in the midst of defining its role on environmental sustainability to bring together people from all walks of life to co-create and educate on the creation a healthier community along all facets of health, leaving a legacy that this community still enjoys.

 Tweet: @givinggreen "Central Y Green Roof"

Summary

Are you a believer now? The key take away is your organization needs to get in gear to become more sustainable and you have the solution that

will allow your organization to further your mission, build visibility, increase your ability to fund-raise, and find free help to get the ball rolling. I will help you build this plan as you read on.

Action Items:

1: Learn, talk, question. Speak to everyone and anyone in your organization to learn about what is already being done to become more sustainable. This could be big things like recycling, or individuals who bike to work. Try to understand how you already are starting to become a more sustainable and environmentally friendly organization. You will build an inventory of what has happened in the past, what worked, what failed and where you should be going.

Your goal is to be the most knowledgeable person in your organization about how your charity relates to sustainability. You should have a clear inventory or list of what has happened. You will be amazed at how green your organization already is. You will also find your allies, future best friends and green teamers!

2. Look around and listen carefully. Future Green Team members are distributed throughout your organization – staff, volunteers, members, clients. Build a list of people that you want to be part of this movement.

3. Tweet your thoughts on @givinggreen "concept" chapter.

Example:

@givinggreen, your concept is miserable, I plan to donate it to charity

@givinggreen, I love your concept and started my research today!

Develop the strength to do bold things, not the strength to suffer.
- Niccolo Machiavelli "The Prince"

There is nothing more uncommon than common sense.
- Frank Lloyd Wright

PART I – Look Before You Leap

I am one of those people that will sit in a meeting, listen to meandering or conceptual conversations for about 5 to 10 minutes and then pop - my hand shoots up and/or I interrupt with a question that usually starts with "I'm sorry, I must not understand why <<insert current topic here>> can't be translated into something meaningful and start to incorporate it immediately <<insert 3 action items that could start today>>." I have little patience for circular conversations, vague direction and double-speak. I pride myself on the ability to listen to conversations, and then develop solutions that are actionable and to start DOING! I'll be honest, at times I move too quickly…but I would rather err on the side of haste than do nothing. I am confident that I will act with compassion, the best intentions, actively seek feedback, and ask forgiveness later.

That being said, there is a time to pause, gather the facts understand what is happening, why it is happening and then chart the course. These next few chapters are about looking around, recognizing what is happening that is successful, looking for opportunities that are easy to change, and identifying challenges. All of these will be part of developing your roadmap. Buckle up, the ride begins now.

There are three types of people in this world: those who make things happen, those who watch things happen and those who wonder what happened.
   - Mary Kay Ash (founder of Mary Kay Cosmetics)

On this path, it is only the first step that counts.
   - St. Jean Baptist-Marie Vianney

Chapter 2 – Defining Your Shade of Green

Understanding where you are is the first step to knowing where you need to go. While working in some degree of chaos is normal for most organizations, you need to have a basic understanding of how your organization works, and the footprint it leaves on the planet. There are myriad of resources that include books, websites and consultants that can provide a detailed evaluation of the ecological footprint, some of which I share later, but it will forever remain a moving target.

The focus of this chapter is geared to be more of a homework assignment, laden with opportunities to learn about sustainability by understanding your organization's lighting, recycling program, water usage, and more. It's a chapter that requires you to get up and look around (at least by the second time you read it.) I will guide you through an initial process to assess your organization, and to move from anecdotal examples to actual information. This approach is to look at the significant impacts first, and then drill down as you get into the inner working of your organization. It will help you to put your finger on the pulse of your charity's environmental health.

For example, looking across the United States in 2010, this chart shows the percentage of how much money was spent on building systems in office buildings. You can see that lighting was over 14%, and the mechanical systems (water and space heating, cooling, refrigeration and ventilation) used more than 50% of the building's energy.

You do not need to be technically inclined to do this assignment, but don't shy away from going outside of your comfort zone! Start with the easy (*) and work toward the more difficult (**). You will definitely need the assistance of someone from the maintenance or property team to discover the technical (***) items (even those who are technically inclined) as the information is specific to the building and its operations. The more you can figure out, the better the picture you can draw.

<u>Now wait</u> – before you skip ahead and decide that this is too technical, or too much detailed work, slow down and imagine yourself back in school. Treat this as an assignment and do this to better your organization and to learn – to better yourself.

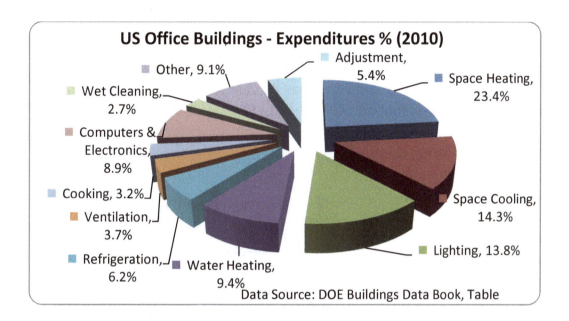

US Office Buildings - Expenditures % (2010)

- Other, 9.1%
- Wet Cleaning, 2.7%
- Computers & Electronics, 8.9%
- Cooking, 3.2%
- Ventilation, 3.7%
- Refrigeration, 6.2%
- Water Heating, 9.4%
- Adjustment, 5.4%
- Space Heating, 23.4%
- Space Cooling, 14.3%
- Lighting, 13.8%

Data Source: DOE Buildings Data Book, Table

Learning New Skills and Pushing your Boundaries

Before the Colorado Avalanche ("Avs") won their back-to-back Stanley Cup Championships in the mid-1990s, it was decided that the Avs needed a new home. This was the Pepsi Center, set in the "golden triangle" of downtown Denver. As a budding young civil engineer that had developed some pretty good skills

Career-Improving Tip:

Knowing how to navigate your organization's hierarchy is important to develop positive momentum. It may be important that you have some discussion with your manager to garner support and work within the organizational effectively. It will also help to create contacts and access to key people within your organization and to avoid stepping on toes.

evaluating structural building systems both in the ground and above, I was selected to run the inspection team overseeing the building of this NHL/NBA arena on behalf of the owner and the City of Denver, and yes, it was a daunting task.

I started off by working with the contractors and other consultants as the site was transformed from a historic (and contaminated) railyard to a parking lot and deep foundation system to hold up this 50,000-seat arena. This project required hundreds of piers to be drilled in to the ground and immense amount of reinforcing steel, structural concrete and masonry – all which needed to be inspected. I developed a great system with the contractors to ensure that everything was done properly without delaying their schedule. Now this was all stuff that I knew well (or learned fast enough that nobody noticed.) But, when it came to the

structural steel inspections - the trusses, beams, columns, bolts and welds - I moved into an area that was completely new to me. We brought in a senior welding inspector and I worked alongside him gleaning his knowledge until I knew it well.

What he couldn't teach me was how to get comfortable with walking along a 4-inch beam 126 feet in the air from connection to connection! That just took time. At first I was terrified and felt pathetic as I scooted along the beam on my butt with my harness dragging behind.

Eventually, I could walk holding the safety wire, and by the end, I was climbing up and down trusses - no bolt was hidden from me as I traversed the steel. I had to keep pushing myself well outside of my comfort zone to keep this project moving along at its aggressive schedule to meet their ambitious deadlines. But, once I broke through my comfort zone, it was exhilarating!

As you start to think about your organization, you will have to learn a lot about how it works to help find solutions. You will tackle things that are new, difficult and outside your comfort zone, but your cause is just and the goal is critical. Find those important people to help you learn what you need, and it's not like you will have to walk a tightrope a hundred feet in the air!

As you start to look at your building, you may start to wonder how one part of the building consumes energy relative to another. This is a simple view to give you a sense of relative scale.

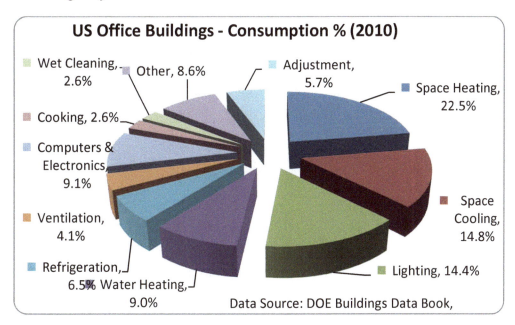

BASIC INFORMATION

Start by gathering some basic data about your organization. I have created an assessment template at www.GivingCharitiesGreen.com/Assessments to help gather this information.

Number of employees (*): If possible, see if you can break it down to full-time and part-time. If you can also determine the typical number of volunteers, note that as well.

Number of sites/locations (*): If you can, get a list of each site name, address, square-footage, type of program(s) you deliver, contact information, whether the site is owned vs. leased. Determine if they have a green team, and capture their contact name and info.

OPERATIONAL INTIATIVES

Dive into your work environment, head office, and areas you and colleagues spend time and work. This potential list is so large, that it is literally endless. You are limited by your imagination.

 Tweet other ideas (@givinggreen "ops checklist")

In the meantime, start with the following, and add more of your own that you discover while asking around:

- **General Recycling in your places of business:**

Are there blue bins for paper (*)?

Does the cleaning staff actually recycle the paper at the end of the day/week (**)? Ask your maintenance person - they'll know. One trick is to see if they have garbage bins and recycling bins in the loading dock or maintenance areas.

Is your organization recycling batteries (*)? Did you know that batteries take up 2-3% of landfills by volume but contribute up to 85% of the hazardous materials in many landfills! This would be a great initiative to start if you don't already have this program in-place!

What happens to old computers and monitors when they are retired (**)? Ask someone in IT - they'll know.

A Word on Vocabulary:

I use "Sustainably Green" as the title of the document that establishes the set of principles or policy. This industry has so much vocabulary with multiple meanings that depends on your experience. In this book:

Green *is used to describe any activity or event that helps to improve the environmental footprint of a person, organization or community by conserving natural resources…not what is in your salad bowl, nor where your putt a golf ball or a feeling of envy - although it occasionally refers to money.*

Environmental *is the most commonly used term for Green. It isn't being used as a term that has historically been attached to hazardous waste (Environmental Cleanup) and is also used to define your surroundings (e.g. work environment).*

- **Printer Paper:**

Check to see if it is FSC Certified and/or has recycled content on the packaging (*).

Are printers settings defaulted to printing double-sided (**)?

- **Recycling in the Kitchen/Eating Areas:**

Is there recycling for paper and plastics (*)?

Is the organic food waste being captured separately (*)?

What types of cups are being used (styrofoam, paper, food based, ceramic/glass, etc) (*)?

- **Look in your Bathrooms & Kitchens:**

Look at the labels on the toilet paper, paper towels, tissue paper – are these products FSC Certified, have an "Eco-logo" and/or contain recycled content (*)?

More on water consumption down below.

- **Meetings:**

Cold Beverages (*): do people typically offer bottled water or water pitchers with glasses? Are you encouraged to bring reusable water bottles?

Hot beverages (*): do people have re-useable cups? Disposable or biodegradable stir sticks? Reuseable mugs?

A Word on Vocabulary
(continued):

Sustainability is used to mean it "…meets the needs of the present without compromising the ability of future generations to meet their own needs." --1987 Brundtland Commission. It is also a term used in businesses referring to the ability to operate continuously in a fiscally responsible manner.

To Go Green is to change your lifestyle intentionally to reduce the negative effects on the environment through your own choices, minimizing your impact on the planet.

Sustainably Green is to "go green" or change your lifestyle intentionally to reduce the negative impacts to the planet to a level that can be carried out without compromising future generations.

Food (*): is it served on washable plates vs. paper or plastic? Is there a culture of fast-food with a lot of packaging or locally grown thoughtfully packaged food?

1. <u>EXISTING GREEN CULTURE</u>

Look at how your programs and/or services operate. Try to understand what existing programs, meetings and events are focused on being green. <u>Anything</u> related to green - regardless of who started it, why it was started, when it was started. It should all be captured and labeled green. This is never an individual effort and green credit should be given to anything that is moving in the right direction (remember that big arrow with the little ones inside from the introduction?). This helps to build goodwill and give accolades to people who started these ideas, as well as build momentum faster. When accounting for existing programs, events or activities that have a green theme, add it to the list!

- Are there any Green Teams, Environmental Teams, or people that are pushing the above types of initiatives (*)? Note how many, where they are located, and try to figure out their outputs and impacts (**). Identify the green leaders (*).

- Do you bring in speakers or companies that have themes related to green topics (*)?

> **Examples of Existing Green Culture:**
>
> At the YMCA, we have an employment program that gives young adults the skills to work in a commercial kitchen. The training program has a focus on the importance of buying local and organic food, food waste composting to keep the smelly material separate, and working with local urban gardeners to teach cultivation and harvesting. These are done for practical reasons with an eye on the environmental impacts.
>
> In the Child Care program, they teach kids about the importance of turning off lights, recycling, and preserving water. The extent of the teaching varies based on the individual Child Care Director. This was later turned into a standardized education program with a free intern that is now used with all kids…see Chapter 12: "Building Momentum with Green Teams" for the rest of the story.
>
> **Dig out these gems!**

- Are there a cleanup days at the local park (*)?

- Are there a bike to work days (*)?

- Do you have bike racks at your site (*)?

- Do you have showers at your office (*)?

- Are there existing programs that address environmental issues (**)? Be creative - they might not have been started to save the world, just to teach or educate people based on their circumstances, and are also ecologically friendly. See **Examples of Existing Green Culture** to see some existing initiatives identified from my research.

2. BUILDING EFFICIENCY:

Explore the world of facilities and building operation and start to understand how your organization's physical assets impact the planet. This gets technical and will be a topic of greater discussion in later chapters. Your ability to understand the efficiency of the building will depend on your knowledge and who you know. Start to figure this stuff out. It will benefit you for the rest of your life at your apartment, house or when battling with the dreaded General Contractor. At this stage of the game, the list below gives some indicators that you can look for to help gauge the level of sustainability in your building. I also get a little more technical on the "back of house" or "boiler room" tours as you dig a bit deeper into the building systems.

As you start, I would recommend you buy your maintenance person a coffee for 15 minutes of their time, and have them help you answer these questions. Coffee is the currency of the construction and maintenance world (while on the clock.)

Electrical Efficiency: Lighting, air-conditioning, and the devices we plug in tend to be the biggest users of electricity. Look for some of these items to get a sense of your building's efficiency:

Basic Lighting (**): Are the round light bulbs in the ceilings, desk lamps or on the walls Compact Fluorescent Lights (CFLs) with a "screw" on the top, or the traditional style (incandescent)? **CFLs generally save 60% electricity and last much longer.** You might even have the extremely efficient LED ones, like on the newer holiday lights. You probably have a combination as LEDs are becoming more affordable and these are even more efficient. Note what you find as indicator that someone is trying to do the right thing, just may not be able to move fast enough because of some barrier. Identify that person as they are part of the existing team that knows what needs to happen and is making it happen!

Fluorescent Lighting (**): Do the rectangular lights in the ceiling (typically fluorescent) have bulbs that are about one inch in diameter - the size of a toilet paper core (if so they are inefficient T12 lights that are no longer even made) or the smaller ½ or ¾-inch bulbs (which are more efficient T5 or T8s)?

Lighting Control (*): do some or all rooms have motion-sensors to turn on the lights?

Convenience and Safety Lighting (*): some lights are always on, like EXIT signs, safety lighting and garage lighting. Pass by your building at night, are the lights on everywhere? Some cleaning companies will turn on all the lights and leave them on while they clean and sometimes after they leave!

Individual Air Conditioning Units (***): Are they old units or new units? You should check the label to see if it says

> **HVAC Defined:**
> Did you know that HVAC stands for **H**eating, **V**entilation, and **A**ir **C**onditioning? The thermostat, sensors and ducts are shared to deliver you warmer or cooler air. The technology that heats up the air (furnace or boiler) and cools down the air (air conditioner or chiller) are where things get more technical.

"Energy Star", "EnerGuide" or not. "Energy Star" means it is newer and more efficient. While you are there, you should see if it contains R-22 or R-410A. R-22, also known as HCFC-22, is the refrigerant that keeps

Level of Task Difficulty

(*) easy   (**) more difficult   (***) technical / maintenance person needed everything cool in older units, but has been phased out due to its ozone-depleting effects. R-410A is the newer "approved" replacement.

Building-wide Air Conditioning (**):
Are there programmable or updated thermostats? Bigger buildings have more complicated systems. A great way to see if you have more efficient systems, regardless of the size of the building, is to look at the thermostat. Updated and efficient systems have programmable thermostats that both sense the space and work intelligently to ensure energy is used appropriately. Older thermostats just go on and off manually and are usually just left on.

Small Appliances (*): Look at the fridge, does it have an "Energy Star" label? Do you have plug-in heaters? Do you have old clunky computers and monitors? Is there a culture of people leaving computers on overnight? Do you have electric baseboard heaters (these are big and inefficient users of electricity) under windows and desks? Are there power-bars at each desk so people can turn off their stations overnight?

Building System Appliances (***): Basement Tour! (…come on, this is fun. If you are weary, think back to the "fun house" tours you took at Halloween or Carnival and take the tour!) If you have been able to have productive conversations with your maintenance person, ask them for a tour of the building through their eyes. They will be delighted to show off this space! Ask them to show you the water heater – is it electrical? If so, does it have an "Energy Star" label?

Ask them to show you other items that use electricity for supporting the building. Most of them will show you a

How Intelligent Is Your Building?

Just as you can stare into the eyes of a stranger and see if there is a light flickering with ideas and questions…or a dim and cloudy vacancy, the building offers its own hints to its acumen.

The thermostat is one of the building's major "senses." If it is 30 years old with a rusty lever, it is likely not too swift! If it has a programmable LCD or display, it is indicative of great things happening elsewhere in the building, maybe even a glimmer of brilliance. Stare into the eyes of your building, what do you see?

computer that was given to them in the 1990s, and never touched again.

 Tweet @givinggreen "old computer" if I'm right!

Gas Efficiency: One of the largest impacts on your organization's ecological and carbon footprint is its gas consumption. Most of the time, gas is used to heat the building's air and water. If you look back at the pie chart at the start of this chapter, you will see that this uses more than half of your energy and half of your spending.

Heating your building's air (**): Are there programmable or updated thermostats? As mentioned above, these systems get increasingly complicated. You don't have to know how they work, just look at the age of the thermostat as an indication. Whatever technology is behind the walls will make the air hotter. As with air conditioning, the heating is usually controlled by sensors or a thermostat. The better the thermostat, the better control the maintenance team has over the building.

Heating your building's air, part 2 (***): To dig deeper, go for a "back-of-house" tour. One rule of thumb that works with heaters and boilers – the smaller the unit, the more efficient (also, the dirtier the older!) Ask your maintenance person their opinion on its efficiency.

Heating your building's water (***): Again, your maintenance person is your friend here. On your tour, ask them to show you the water heater. Is it gas? If so, does it have an "Energy Star" label? Ask them to show you other equipment that uses gas for supporting the building. Are they new? Do they have "Energy Star" labels?

> **_Wasteful Facts:_**
> _Water_ – A single leaky faucet or shower head that drips at the rate of one drip per second can waste more than 3,000 gallons (11,300 Liters) per year...that's 100 soaks in the tub.
> _Light_ – A single 100W incandescent bulb left on for a year will cost about $100 and will use 876 kWh. That is enough to power a typical house for close to a month!

- Water Efficiency: Most people appreciate the natural resource that is water and the need to use what you need – not be wasteful. What many people don't realize is the amount of energy used by major systems to get that water into your building. There are pumps, filters, chemical treatment stations, pipes, more pumps, valves – and that just gets it to your water-consuming appliance. Conserving water not only protects this importance resource, it saves a lot of energy.

For faucets and showers, they are typically rated based on their flowrate in gallons or liters per minute (GPM/LPM). For toilets and urinals, they are rated based on the gallons/liters per flush (GPF/LPF)…and when you opened this book today, I bet you didn't think you would be learning about urinals!

So, how do you figure out if you are being efficient or inefficient? One of the tricks that I recommend is the get yourself a Starbucks Grande Coffee (it holds 16oz). If you can't find the label on your water-using appliance, see how long it takes to fill it up! Refer to the "Starbuck Cup Trick" inset for a description of how it works.

> ### *Starbucks Cup Trick:*
> *While this may appear to be a piece of shameless promotion, I actually created this trick after a walk along the Newfoundland Atlantic Coast. As I finished my trek back from the Signal Hill, I picked up a Grande Americano in St. Johns, and then walked back to my hotel to work on this section. I was trying to figure out the efficiency of the sink in my hotel room, and I couldn't see any labels. I rinsed my cup out for a drink of water, and voila, this trick was born!*
>
> *It is simple, and relies on a 16-ounce cup, or a Starbucks Grande. It works best with faucets and shower heads – not so much on toilets!*
>
> ***Step 1:*** *Place cup under spout.*
> ***Step 2:*** *While looking at your watch, turn on and count the seconds.*
> ***Step 3:*** *When your hand gets wet (i.e. water overflows the rim), record the amount of seconds:*
> - *less than 3 sec = not efficient*
> - *3 sec = 9.5 LPM (2.5 GPM)*
> - *5 sec = 8 LPM (1.5 GPM)*
> - *15 sec = 2 LPM (0.5 GPM)*
>
> *If you get four seconds, it is likely a 2.5 GPM faucet with some grunge inside, making it even more efficient!*

Faucets (*): Do they leak? Do they have auto-flush sensors? Are they low-flow? (it's usually written on the side of the round section – right where the water flows out) 9.5 LPM (2.5 GPM) is the current standard for "low flow." Can't tell? Use the Starbucks Cup Trick.

Shower heads (*): Are they low-flow models? Low flow is 9.5 LPM (2.5 GPM). Can't tell? Again, use the Starbucks Cup Trick.

Toilet (*): Look carefully - are they dual flush or low-flow and/or have auto-flush sensors? Typical low flow for toilets is 6 LPF or 1.6 GPF. The label is on the back of the bowl…careful now, I said look! If you can't tell - flush the toilet. Does the flow go on and on? This indicates a high-flow or inefficient toilet. Does it stop after two seconds? This is low flow, probably 6 LPF (1.6 GPF)? There are also 5 LPF (1.3 GPF) toilets available too. Older toilets can use up to 26.5 LPF (7 GPF)! At this point, note if your building's toilets are high or low-efficiency.

Urinals (*): from a distance…you never want to actually touch a urinal, right? Are they low-flow and/or have auto-flush sensors? A water efficient urinal is 3.8 LFP or 1 GPF or less (older ones use 11 liters or 3 gallons!) Not sure? Move on!

Handwash (*): <u>Seriously, please wash your hands</u> after assessing your building's water efficiency - with soap (*)! This is a good use of water.

- <u>Cleaning Chemicals</u> (*): While you are bending the ear of your maintenance person, ask them about their cleaning chemicals:

Are they marked with "Eco-Logo" or "Green Seal" certifications (*)? As an example, bleach is not considered a "green" chemical by these two certifications. Just note if yes, no, or a combination.

- <u>Hazardous Chemicals</u> (**): This is a question that is often sensitive, but ask your maintenance person about old chemicals on unlabeled pails. If there are "unknown" items, ask your service contractor to a take a look. I believe in amnesty for honesty – help them find a good solution. It's better to solve this problem with an eye to safety than let someone pour it down the drain.

- <u>Building Exterior</u> (***): As you gaze through the recently washed windows and doors around your building, you are also staring at the weakest point for keeping your building warm in the winter and cold in the summer. Are your windows double pane (i.e. two sheets of glass) or even triple-paned? The more glass the better. Do you notice a "foggy" window? – that means it is doing very little insulation work. Other areas to look for wasted heat and air conditioning are the doors and walls. Are your doors drafty? Are there obvious warm and cold spots? There are all good things to note, and your maintenance person will have a good idea on well-insulated the building is. In cooler climates, a good rule of thumb is if you see lots of heaters under desks or in offices, that you are dealing with an insulation problem and wasting lots of energy.

3. UNDERLINE INFORMATION TECHNOLOGY (IT):

While the lighting technology that we use is over 130 years old, much of the technology industry moves at even faster pace. Many of us remember TVs and computers being introduced to the world as we grew up – depending on the true color of your hair – if you still have it! While the size of our mobile phones and PDAs get smaller, their capabilities grow exponentially.

The main systems that run the brains of this information network: servers, switches, and computers are much more efficient. Even more impactful is the design of the IT architecture with centralized application servers, virtualized servers and shared centralized storage systems. THIS CAN HAVE A VERY SIGNIFICANT IMPACT. There are significant costs wasted each year because of the outdated technology choices that charities (and businesses) make that cost extra money and resources to run, repair, keep the servers cool, and even the time and gas for technicians to visit your sites for the "IT Support." Some offices can spend 5 to 10% of their energy load on computers and related equipment (source DOE, buildings energy data book.)

I believe this to be important enough, that I have dedicated an entire chapter on this: **Chapter 14 – Improving Your Information Technology Systems**, to assist with understanding some of the current choices and pitfalls, written by a guest author – the IT guy for the IT guys!

For this assessment stage, there are some leading questions that will help you understand where your organization stands on the spectrum of computer efficiency.

IT people also love a cup of coffee, and are critical to the success of understanding how your IT systems work…just don't bring the coffee into the server room! Please remember that your IT person might be frustrated about the type of system that is being used. While you may discover that the systems are quite outdated, this is more often about the IT department not getting enough money to upgrade their systems. So as you have these conversations, do so with an understanding that you seek to help bring focus to inefficient systems that could improve their budgets.

- Computers (*): Look around your desk. How old is your computer? Is your monitor is really big one that weighs 50 pounds or the new thinner and lighter ones? The newer ones use much less power and work with more modern and efficient computers.

- Servers (**): With the help of your IT person, ask to peek in on the server room. Look around and talk with them about the following things:

- Do the servers look like big computers, sitting on shelves and desks? If so, they are really old.

- Are the servers lined up like a stack of pizza boxes in neat racks? This is newer.

- Are the servers in the racks with lots of gaps? This could be the same as the last one, with fewer servers. Or, it could be a sign that there are modern "blade" servers that are more efficient, but create more heat and need more space to keep cool. Ask them.

- Ask about virtualization, where they take a physical servers (one of the pizza boxes), and put five to ten "virtual servers" (virtual pizza boxes) onto one physical server. This demonstrates a modern IT approach that is very efficient, and has many other benefits to the IT team as well around data recovery and network speed.

- Is the server room uncomfortably hot? If so, this can burn out the equipment more quickly, create data loss and start to create other issues. While they might be saving energy, this is not the way to do it.

- IT Architecture (***): As you start to discuss the architecture of the IT systems, this starts to get very technical. There are some trends you are trying to understand with these questions about how things are set up.

- Does each site run with its own servers? Or is everything centrally managed?

- Are we managing our disaster recovery? Could this be done offsite by a partner?

Benchmark

Aren't you curious how your organization compares to other ones? Once you are done, you can use a free test for your organization at www.GivingCharitiesGreen.com/shade-o-meter to see your shade of green. After answering 25 questions, it will assign a value that gives you a starting point for your shade of green.

Summary

Okay, that was some real work, but you have now immersed yourself (or at least thought about immersing yourself) into your organization's current state of affairs. Are you surprised at how much you are doing to be greener? Most people are, and part of the problem is, nobody else knows all the work that is being done or the willingness to get it done. Some organizations are halfway there, the steps taken have been done in isolation and not many people know.

The above research expedition will now be the foundation for your next step. Celebrate completing your first step…go buy yourself another coffee, or maybe even a latte!

Action Items:

1. **If you did all of your homework and completed your Initial Assessment Form on www.GivingCharitiesGreen.com/Assessments, you get a free pass.**

If not, you should take the time to understand where you are now, before you start to create change. You can try out your delegation skills or volunteer recruitment abilities. Find a student or a friend to help you work on completing this necessary step. You can act as their advisor and they can track down the answers. You can divide and conquer. Be creative…this is an important milestone.

2.   Make sure you take the quick survey to define your organization's "Shade of Green." Is your organization lime-green or chartreuse? There is a 25-question survey that determines your shade at www.GivingCharitiesGreen.com/shade-o-meter

3.   Tweet your thoughts, or additional checklist items to:

   @givinggreen "ops checklist

The successful person makes a habit of doing what the failing person doesn't like to do.
>   - Thomas Edison

If one advances confidently in the direction of his dreams, and endeavors to live the life which he has imagined, he will meet with success unexpected in common hours. He will put some things behind, will pass an invisible boundary; new universal, and more liberal laws will begin to establish themselves around and within him.
>   - Henry David Thoreau, "Walden"

Try not. Do or do not, there is no try.
>   - Yoda

Chapter 3 – Demand Change

I loved the movie, "Jerry Maguire." Tom Cruise played the passionate change manager who has a sudden moral epiphany and then works tirelessly as he prepares his Mission Statement to demand change. You need to channel Jerry Maguire – feel his passion. Just as it consumed him, you need to ignite your passion from within to propel you forward. Passion is infectious. **A well-organized, articulate and passionate leader is unstoppable.**

You are now at a cross-road. If you have completed your action items from the last two chapters, know some of the things your organization is doing and have a sense of what can be done. This last stage of learning and understanding can take a few days or up to a few weeks. You might even know some people who are ready to join your plan of making your charity Sustainably Green – now is your time to get noticed and start the change!

Armed with your research, you have to convince your organization that this needs to happen today ("help me, help you"), that you understand your organization and that your plan will enhance your organization's mission, drive additional donations and volunteerism and get your green on. When your CFO says "Show me the money!" you will show her or him that being Sustainably Green will bring money, volunteers, profile and more. You want her to say "You had me at 'Hello'", or even better "With your well-organized and thoughtful plan, *you complete me*."

After you have taken some time to see what has been done in your organization (**Chapter 2: Defining Your Shade of Green**), you should find natural points of synergy between what your charity does and potential sustainability initiatives. At the YMCA of Greater Toronto, in 2007, our Vision was: Making Connections: Strong Kids, Strong Families, Strong Communities. We used "strong communities" as the driver that actually includes the environment and its use in a sustainable way.   Here is an excerpt from my "Mission Statement" for the "Green Fund" that I introduced in **Chapter 1: The Concept and Why this Works**:

"At the center of the YMCA Vision is the concept of connecting with the community. This concept permeates every aspect of our Strategic Plan. That everyone involved in the YMCA is a part of the community, is implicit. Our members and staff, championed by the youth, have challenged the definition of community to include the environment. In addition, the Core Values of 'Health' and 'Responsibility' call out for green solutions and the concept of environmental stewardship."

You need to find the core drivers within your organization and dovetail the environmental stewardship into this message. Understand this, articulate this and write your call to action - plant your seed for change.

Here is another excerpt from my "Green Fund" proposal:

"Moving good intent into action is the trick with all things successful in life. We have moved in this direction in fits and spurts over the last many years. We need to turn the pressure full-on and create a sustainable current that captures our Association in force.

There are many low-cost green initiatives that are building momentum in our Association today. We are starting to reduce paper usage in our offices, offer bicycle parking, use biodegradable cups, recycle better, etc. The Procurement Team that helps us find vendors and suppliers has been blending green into the services and products they make available to staff and our members through their strong leadership.

The facilities offer some of the greatest opportunities for conservation and the use of alternate energy sources; they also offer the greatest barriers.

The hardest part of moving from an inefficient building to one that has been renewed with a sustainable approach, is the upfront capital costs.

(you should be chanting "Show me the money!")

[With the "Green Fund"] the key message to send to potential donors is that they will invest in the preservation of the environment in their local community, the conservation of resources in their region and support their charity (us) to build stronger, smarter and better people in their neighborhood. This is the green gift that keeps giving.

The full version of this "Green Fund" proposal document is available on the website www.GivingCharitiesGreen.com/Resources. You can refer to these ideas as you develop your own call to action - your own Mission Statement.

The impact was immediate within my organization. I was asked to help lead this Association-wide "Environmental Sustainability" initiative for YMCA of Greater Toronto. It was clear that I was passionate, motivated, and knowledgeable and had the start of a plan to drive change. The appetite was there, we were falling behind, and I was ready to lead the change. Your turn…set this in motion.

 Tweet @givinggreen "show me the money" if you agree and want to make change!

Fear of Change:

"Fear itself is quite fear-inducing. Most intelligent people in the world dress it up as something else: optimistic denial." Tim Ferriss (Four Hour Work Week, 2007, USA, Crown Publishing)

Most people live their lives in some form of ignorant bliss. Some people do nothing as they are hopelessly optimistic that things will work out; others, do nothing as they don't think they will effect change. If you are in one of these camps, slap yourself…shake off those self-deprecating useless mental thoughts and utter waste of your life's energy. If you are still having anxiety about putting pen to paper, crafting a "call-to-action" and articulating your thoughts to the senior people in your organization, watch the YouTube video "The Most Terrifying Video You'll Ever See." It is a really well-organized argument by science teacher Greg Craven who has given a simple argument about to act or not to act. His 10-minute video post has led to many other posts and conversations, but the simplicity of his argument is demonstrated in a simple grid that shows the impact of different possibilities of responding the effects of climatic change. To act or not to act…and each decision is either true or false. Easy peasy.

Here are your options:

To act: If you create a Mission Statement and present it to your colleagues, the outcome could be that they don't think that it will work for your organization. However, they might also think of you as a passionate person who is motivated and could be a future leader. On the other hand, **if you act and your colleagues agree, you might have created an exciting new career where will gain firsthand experience and play a leading role in moving our world to become more sustainable.**

Not act: If you don't act, and this is all a "big hoax" and fabricated, as some politicians still actually believe, then you lost nothing…except that you are reading this book, clearly have some passion about the world we live in, and by not acting, you will lose the chance to take some meaningful action. Make the right choice!

Action Items:

1. Get politically savvy and understand your organization's plans. Study the Executive Team, read the strategic and operational plans, learn who is the one that others rely on to get things done. (Hint: it is the busiest person.) Keep your eyes and ears open and get to know the Executive Team, and let them get to know you.

2. Think, watch and write. You need to take your ideas and build a call to action. You need to write a clear message to your CEO or Executive Director that demonstrates your knowledge, your passion, your willingness to get the job done and an outline of how you will do it. You need to do the research that shows you are organized. You need to show the way.

Your goal is to be heard and to have someone be appointed as your Executive Sponsor and Executive Team contact, to be your mentor and interact with the Executive Team.

Tools: Gather your research, and look for trends in what your organization is doing and planning to do.

Review your corporate documents and list the points of synergy that you identified. Example, is health mentioned in your Strategic Plan? Huge point of synergy! Improving the health of people in our communities is not possible without fresh air to breathe, clean water to drink, and fresh, locally-grown food to eat. Use your imagination.

Review the full version of the "Green Fund" document to draw parallels to your organization.
www.GivingCharitiesGreen.com/Resources

Use the presentation I have prepared to demonstrate your points.
www.GivingCharitiesGreen.com/Resources

3. Make your pitch. Don't make it perfect, but make it great. Get in front of the Executive Team and make them believe that you know your organization, you have some great people thinking about solutions, you have the outline of a plan, and you are seeking their support. Make a difference. Make your pitch.

4. Are you ready? Say it out loud! Tweet your thoughts to:

 @givinggreen "Demand Change" (e.g. I will "demand change"!)

5. After your pitch, tweet:

 @givinggreen "pitch":   "they said Yes" or "they said No

As to methods there may be a million and then some, but principles are few. The man who grasps principles can select his own methods. The man who tries methods, ignoring principles, is sure to have trouble.

> *- Ralph Waldo Emerson*

If you have built castles in the air, your work need not be lost; that is where they should be. Now put the foundations under them.
> *- Henry David Thoreau, "Walden"*

Don't take no for an answer, never submit to failure. Do not be fobbed off with mere personal success or acceptance. You will make all kinds of mistakes, but as long as you are generous and true, and also fierce, you cannot hurt the world or even seriously distress her. She was made to be wooed and won by youth.
> *- Winston Churchill*

Chapter 4 - Developing your Organization's "Sustainably Green" Principles

Getting the green light to move ahead comes in many forms. Once you have some form of approval, you are out of the gate. Be the optimist, push boundaries. If you haven't received negative feedback, treat that as implicit positive feedback and agreement. If you received a no, or more likely, "we're not yet convinced", don't give up – as Winston Churchill says, "don't take no for an answer". Get some support, listen carefully to the feedback, and try a different angle. Get to yes!

The next step is to define the principles for your organization. How does becoming "Sustainably Green" look in your organization? What are your points of connection for how you can extend your mission while achieving a healthier planet? This chapter is a nuts and bolts discussion that will give you ideas and help your prepare your set of principles (and for some, an "Environmental Policy"). It can get a bit technical at times, but stay focused – your goal is to build a draft document that will be reviewed by all sorts of people that will offer feedback and help to move this towards a more refined vision.

Establishing your "Sustainably Green Principles" will help your organization define what is important and then give you the guidelines for building an implementation plan. Defining these principles will be a great chance to re-engage your Green Team members and create a first major task. The initial focus should be to reduce your charity's "Environmental Footprint" – the way each organization impacts the environment, uses resources and educates the next generation. The footprint that each organization leaves varies based in size, number of buildings, types of activities, and number of people.

As you work through this section, you need to stay focused and motivated – here is one of experiences that helps to drive me.

Finding Your Inner Motivation: Converting Child Labor into a Camp Experience

As a young teenager living in New England in the 80s, I was constantly being introduced to outdoor experiences on family vacations. With five kids, camping is cheap and nature is timeless. One such adventure was to a "Family Camp" at Winona Camp in Bethel, Maine. Along the shores of Moose Pond, my love for the outdoors and a deep appreciation for nature was rooted. After 10 days of exploring the woods, enjoying water activities in kayaks, canoes, sailboats, rock-climbing and all the other activities offered at the outdoor camp, I came to the realization that I needed to go to this camp. I needed to leave my family at home and be the outdoorsman that I knew I had to become. But alas, after discussions with my parents, I learned that camp was too expensive. My family could not afford this for one or two months, and like the rocks we skipped along the water's surface, my dreams sank.

At the ripe old age of 13, I decided that I controlled my future and I would find my own solution. First, I negotiated with my parents that if I could pay for half of the cost through hard work, they would find the other half to support my dream. My options were few to generate enough money to meet my half of the bargain. My current paper route, shoveling snow and cutting lawns could only get me so far, and only at 15 would they let me be a bagboy down at the local supermarket...these child labor laws are getting in the way of my dreams!

As I approached the following summer and as my future friends were readying themselves for their summer on the shores of Moose Pond, I exploited a loophole in the child-labor rules – I could work as a farm hand at a nearby commercial tobacco farm. As an awkward 14-year-old with white-blonde hair and fair skin, I boarded the bus at the north edge of Hartford, Connecticut and watched as we weaved through the inner streets of Hartford through the poorest sections of our region as my fellow farm workers (mainly black men aged 30 to 50) joined the yellow school bus to the eventual terminus at the local tobacco farm.

I spent the summer picking leaves from early morning to mid-afternoon, and actually had green thumbs (along with all of my other fingers.) As my future friends learned camp songs and gained skills in navigating the Allagash River, I was learning traditional Jamaican songs from the farm laborers that worked the Eastern seaboard harvesting the farms and sending their hard-earned money back to the families they left at home.

As marshmallows were being roasted at campfires, I was drinking warm Tang and eating my homemade bologna sandwiches that were always too warm from the intense summer heat (I have never had Tang or bologna since that summer!) On Fridays, we always stopped at the Check Cashing station where we would all exit the bus, and convert our weekly toil to cash (except that many converted theirs to brown paper bags at the adjacent liquor store.) My education deepened as I realized how lucky I was.

Each Saturday I dutifully deposited my hard-earned money at the bank and grew the savings account to exceed my half of the cost to go to Camp Winona for the full summer the following year - and what a summer that next year was! The bus that I boarded this time headed north to Camp Winona and it was better than I could have hoped: I learned to rock-climb, canoe river rapids, kayak (and do an Eskimo roll!) I became a Junior Maine Guide in record time and I was even chosen for one of the top camper awards.

The experience that I gained through both summers have affected my life to this day and the dividends that it paid were all unexpected as it became a pivotal stepping stone in my life for three reasons:

➢ I learned that I could accomplish something that I wanted and am passionate about. That built incredible self-motivation and self-confidence.

➢ I proved to others that I was motivated, determined and patient. That opened doors that I didn't know existed.

➢ I learned an appreciation for the environment and to love nature for its purity, biodiversity, and variety of experiences. Nature gives strength to everyone who uses it with no strings attached.

As you look ahead to understand the impact that you want to make, remember that while you are working toward a goal that you see, the dividends that you will be paid are often not even known and the doors that you don't even know exist will open.

Let's take your motivation and passion, and build a document that starts defines your organization's approach to being "Sustainably Green." There are many drivers that should be considered when defining your organization's "Environmental Footprint", some of the most common ones are presented below. These principles should be developed in a way that shouldn't need to be updated every year. Pairing this with an annual "Implementation Plan" (discussed in **Chapter 5: Getting Your Organization Organized**) will allow you to build short-term goals that are consistent with your organization's principles.

Factors that define a Charity's Environmental Footprint: This is written in a way that you can take these items and use in your final "Sustainably Green Principles" or "Environmental Policy." An editable version of this section is available on the website at www.GivingCharitiesGreen.com/Resources. These are the basis of what we used to develop the one for the YMCA of Greater Toronto, but are sufficiently generic that they can be transferred to any organization. Just pick these ala carte and build into your "Sustainably Green Principles:"

Energy Management: Reducing the energy used in our buildings to heat and cool them, power the equipment, heat the water, and power the computers and lighting is the largest contributor to carbon footprint reduction. *(This is where you will actually save a lot of money and drive contributions.)*

Waste Management: Minimizing the amount of waste sent to landfills is a top priority. Reduction, reuse and recycling are the preferred methods of waste minimization; however, when solid waste cannot be eliminated, there is commitment to careful management and disposal.

Emission Control: Globally, there is scientific consensus that the amount of greenhouse gases in our atmosphere has reached critical levels. In addition, other forms of gases pollute our neighborhoods and waterways. It is of vital importance that we reduce our carbon footprint and adapt to the impacts of climate change.

Sustainable Resource Management: Preserving our natural resources by reducing and reusing in innovative ways to drive down continued overconsumption should be a focus.

Renewable Energy Sources: Harnessing natural and sustainable energy to supplement the other forms of energy we consume will make up a portion of our energy use. *(Remember: conservation ALWAYS precedes alternate forms of energy generation.)*

Sustainably Produced Products: Searching for products that are made of sustainable materials, whether they are recycled or are made from sustainable resources.

Water Usage: Reducing water consumption at the source within building systems as well as drinking water and irrigation.

Natural Spaces: Reclaiming and enhancing natural spaces across the buildings and properties we own, lease, operate and visit in a way that promotes biodiversity and improved health of its users.

Next, what does each of these factors look like within your organization?

Once you have defined the key elements that contribute to your "Environmental Footprint", you need to express how you will translate these concepts into key commitments. These commitments should be specific and provide the basis for future measurement and can be inserted under the above headings.

Some examples are shown below:

Energy Management:

- Reduce our overall energy use below our baseline year by 30% by the year 2020.
- Fund and implement energy-saving techniques and processes within our operations.
- Use high-efficiency fixtures, appliances and equipment in our renovations and future development.

- Encourage our vendors to provide energy-efficient products by adding criteria for energy use, where appropriate to our procurement policies.
- Participate in community energy-reduction programs.

Waste Management:

- Reduce the amount of waste we send to landfill below our baseline year by 40% by the year 2020.
- Recycle paper, cardboard, glass, plastic and metal throughout the organization.
- Dispose of electronic equipment and devices in an environmentally-responsible manner, including computers, ink cartridges, cell phones, batteries.
- Promote the reuse of furniture and other fixtures to reduce the amount of materials going to landfill.
- Properly recycling and/or disposing of hazardous materials.
- Increasing the use of recyclable products will reduce the amount of waste that is sent to landfill.

Emission Control:

- Reduce our overall greenhouse gas emissions below our baseline year by 65% by 2020 and be carbon neutral by 2040.*{{ Footnote: should you become successful in selling your carbon credits, then you can change this to "sell more credits that we generate by 2040." }}
- Promote the use of alternatives to travel, including public transportation and teleconferencing.
- Offset our carbon emissions through renewable energy opportunities.
- Reduce the amount of toxins and volatile organic compounds (VOCs) released into the atmosphere.
- Increase the use of environmentally-friendly cleaning products in our facilities in order to reduce the quantity of hazardous substances released in wastewater.

Sustainable Resource Management: Renewable Energy Sources:

- Identify opportunities for the use of solar, geothermal, biomass and wind power to reduce our dependence on the electrical grid and reduce our greenhouse gas emissions.

Sustainably Produced Products:

- Increase the percentage of sustainably-produced and recycled products (e.g. paper, plastic, building materials) across our Association.
- Include these guidelines into our procurement policies to ensure our vendors are inline with our commitment to environmental responsibility.

Water Usage:

- Reduce the use of water in our facilities below our
- Baseline year by 35% by 2020.
- Encourage the use of reusable water containers and water coolers or tap water in our premises.
- Encourage our larger suppliers to conserve water by adding criteria for water use, where appropriate, to our procurement procedures.

Natural Spaces:

- Enhance or restore 15% or XXX acres of our owned spaces by the year 2020. *(You need to know the amount of land area you own or control.)*
- Protect, restore and enhance local biodiversity by understanding and working with native species to improve the health of our environment.

> **Leadership in Energy and Environmental Design (LEED)** is a points driven evaluation system that gives credits based on environmentally friendly strategies used in building construction, operation & maintenance. LEED standards establish a consistent approach for those who wish to pursue green buildings. In addition, LEED aims to improve occupant well-being, environmental performance and economic returns of buildings, using established and innovative practices, standards and technologies. To learn more, visit

Create a draft outline and shape it with your colleagues and volunteers.

As you start to share ideas, a clear list or priorities will emerge. It can seem a bit scary to select the amount of energy, water or emissions to reduce (e.g. Reduce our overall energy use below our baseline year by 30% in the year 2020.) As you look at your organization, think about how your organization uses these items. For the YMCA, we have huge pools, and showers that run all the time, so we placed a focus on water reduction. We also had a lot of old buildings that were starting to need upgrades, so we focused on energy reduction. It is important to pick your top priorities, and then as you seek additional help, you can refine these numbers. Pick something to create focus and adjust later (see **Analysis Paralysis.)** In the next chapter, we will discuss the baseline year, and you can start to think about the relative percentages that might be appropriate for your organization.

You will then need to think about the principles for how your organization will implement a plan to reduce your "Environmental Footprint" – the "Implementation Plan" that is discussed in **Chapter 5: Getting Your Organization Organized** will help you build this plan. At this stage, you need to think about the principles that align with you Charity's existing principles to ensure you are approaching this with a community-minded lens. Some important ones to consider:

> ***Analysis Paralysis:***
>
> *Do not strive for perfection when developing plans and commitments. These will change as your learn more and you can correct course as time marches on. This same logic applies to measuring your successes. State your assumptions and keep moving. Getting lost in the minutiae and seeking perfection will lose momentum and serve no purpose. Focus on the right direction, not hitting the specific target...I give you permission to be wrong!*

Community-Minded Organization: Become an environmentally-responsible organization does not come from just a reduction of our environmental footprint. There are many other actions that will drive this change and we will strive to identify and implement a balanced approach. These include:

- Incorporate volunteerism into every initiative

- Have educational elements built into every activity and project, including legacy signage to help to tell the story. *(Remember, the journey is equally as important as the destination, make sure you leave signs along the side of the road to help others follow.)*

- Encourage youth of all ages to be included

- Create opportunities for all persons with disabilities.

- Be socially inclusive of the diverse people and cultures that are represented in and around our communities.

Volunteerism: As a charity, we will involve volunteerism at every level to advance our goal to drive behavioral change in our communities. We will create opportunities for volunteers to be included on individual projects, to be associated with specific locations, and support the overall Association's goals to become "Sustainably Green."

We will develop, maintain, and communicate effective procedures, standards and guidelines for our business activities, to learn from and educate our staff, volunteers, members and stakeholders about environmental issues.

Health and Wellness: We will develop and implement our initiatives with consideration for the health of our staff, members, clients, volunteers and community. We will ensure that the installation and long-term impacts of any initiatives provide a net improvement in the physical environment that we affect.

Compliance: We will manage all aspects of our Association to ensure environmental laws and regulations are met with or exceeded. This compliance will apply across all fields: greenhouse gas emissions, energy use, water use, waste management and renewable energy sources. When laws or regulations are not in place, we will maintain best practices within our industry.

Certifications: As we move into new spaces, we will construct new buildings or leased spaces that achieve a LEED (see inset - LEED) standard of Silver or Gold.

Measurement & Monitoring: All actions taken to reduce our environmental footprint will be measured against our baseline year. In the coming years, we will compare our environmental footprint to our baseline year and calculate our reduction in terms of a percentage. Our footprint will be measured across several different categories, including: energy management, waste management, emission control and sustainable resource management. These metrics will be monitored on an annual basis.

The measurement of our environmental footprint will culminate in an annual Environmental Responsibility Report.

Action Items:

Draft your organization's Sustainably Green Principles using the ideas above. An editable template is available at our website www.GivingCharitiesGreen.com. Work with your existing green team to hash out these choices. Have fun - this is an exciting time for your organization. You are documenting how your organization will make a difference.

Use the Presentation template to capture your thoughts and be able to share these ideas with others. www.GivingCharitiesGreen.com/Resources

Tweet your thoughts, or additional checklist items to:

 @givinggreen "green categories

The difference between what we do and what we are capable of doing would suffice to solve most of the world's problem.

 - *Mahatma Gandhi*

Know the rules well, so you can break them effectively.
 - *Dalai Lama XIV*

Chapter 5 – Getting Your Organization Organized

When Martin Luther King gave his "I Have A Dream" speech on the steps of the Lincoln memorial, he captured the world with a simple message of a colorblind society. While many remember the images from his speech made as part of the "March on Washington" in 1963, it was not only the timing that leveraged the suffering and hard work of many up to that day, but his passion and charisma that created an unstoppable resonance throughout the country.

As you look to drive cultural change within your organization, you should know that the timing is right, and all that is needed is a passionate person (that's you) to demonstrate a clear message to incite change. The timing is right because there is a ground swell of activity: Al Gore's "An Inconvenient Truth" hit a chord and resonated; the Intergovernmental Panel on Climate Change (IPCC) has demonstrated clear evidence of the impacts and envisioned futures; governments are trying to motivate individuals and corporations to act more sustainably (some better than others); the effects of climatic change are more evident in recent years; organizations and individuals are starting to move; there is a buzz.

Stages of Change:

One of my mentors, Jim, explained the theory of the "stages of change" to me some years back…and it has stuck with me through many transitions. From small changes, like skipping the morning donut and not using single-use water bottles, to big decisions, like spending two years writing a book! The model is called the Transtheoretical Stages of Change based on the research from James O. Prochaska
at the University of Rhode Island in 1977.

There are six stages:

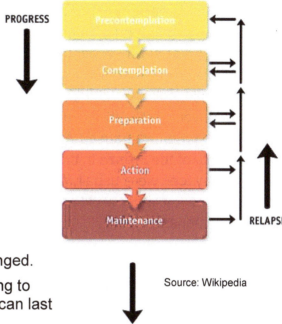

Source: Wikipedia

Pre-contemplation – people are not aware of the concept nor ready to change.

Contemplation – people are aware of the concept, but not ready to change.

Preparation – people are ready to change and are getting ready to start.

Action – people have made a change and their behavior is changed.

Maintenance – people are working to prevent a relapse, a stage which can last indefinitely.

Termination – people will no longer revert back to the old behavior, change complete.

Your task is to find and build internal support throughout your organization and beyond. As you are speaking with different people or groups, remember that they are in one of these stages of change, and your goal is to advance them towards action and eventual termination, at which point your job is done.

Finding Your Inspiration:

One of the first times that I remember appreciating the outdoors as a boy was cross-country skiing with my father. At the crack of dawn on a winter weekend morning, we would head out to the local reservoir lands in suburban Connecticut. As a child, I had always enjoyed playing in the outdoors during our many hikes, camping trips or park adventures, but I have clear and fond memories of the winter adventures that took us into areas that seemed uncharted and pure.

There was a magical transition that would start with the two of us pulling into the parking lot, pulling on our thin leather ski shoes, strapping on the narrow skis and setting out. For the first twenty minutes, I would be stuck in my head, trying to fend off the cold, wondering if I could keep up the pace and begin to slowly separate from civilization. At some point, we might scare a rabbit or some other creature into the brush and all of a sudden I would look around and realize that we were completely alone – no sign of anyone or anything but a beautiful serene winter forest wonderland. When we paused we would only hear ourselves breathing, a gentle whistle of the breeze in the trees, and an overwhelming silence. At that point, my toes were usually frozen, and my heart would warm to this incredible time my father and I share...leaving only our tracks and taking only our memories.

It never ceased to amaze me how we could lose three hours on these days, returning to the car exhausted, yet invigorated. As I cried in anguish as the blood returned to my feet, my father would detour to a nearby Dunkin' Donuts for a hot chocolate and two warm cinnamon buns to literally ice the sweet cake of the morning we just enjoyed. Those were special times for many reasons, but they planted the seeds of my deep appreciation for the power of nature.

As you engage the people in your organization, share your points of inspiration and seek theirs. It is a great way to start a conversation from a place of shared inspiration and work towards a shared solution.

Building Internal Support:

As with any plan you start to communicate, you have to know your audience. Take a look at how your charity is organized so you can develop a plan to reach each group. You are empowered with executive support; now, you need to lead the expedition. As you come up with a plan to have formal and informal meetings to learn about the groups and get your message across, there are three primary goals of this process you should consider:

To communicate the Sustainably Green Principles, seeking their feedback.

To assemble a complete list of what has been done and what could be done.

Identify people that will help you become successful.

Support Teams: Understand the departments that support your organization, and for smaller organizations, many of the roles from these multiple departments combined into a few overwhelmed people. Just think, you have fewer people to interview!

For larger organizations, typical examples include:

Human Resources

Information Technology (IT)

Finance/Accounting

Communications

Procurement

Facilities/Asset Management

Fundraising

Legal/Risk Management

Dress for Success:
 A classic executive coaching book "Dress for Success" by John T. Molloy was released as a new and improved version in 2007. Find an appropriate outfit to show off a green tie, or scarf for the ladies as you delve into your organization. Too formal? Put on a green shirt or a green dress. Have fun with your green persona!

As you have a conversation with each group to learn about what they are doing, you will use that opportunity to explain how it is possible to intentionally become a more sustainable organization that their help is needed, and they play an important role in its success. Your script will look like:

What types of activities have been done in your area that reduces our impact on the environment? (Congratulate them for their successes and write down their activities.)

What else are you planning to do right now?   This is work to be done in existing budget plans.

What else could be done in your area, if you had funding or executive support?

What else could be done in other areas? Remember that they have different relationships, experiences, and perspectives throughout the organization. Go through each support team and program team to draw out their ideas.

Would you like to participate on a Green Team to help look assess our building and then start to make real changes? Keep lists and build a binder with tabs for each department - you will need this soon.

Service-Delivery or Programming Management Teams: Look at how these groups are organized, when they meet, and who puts together their agenda. You goal is to learn about them, get their ideas and implant your ideas about becoming Sustainably Green. I would recommend you approach each leader individually to perform the same type of meeting as with the Support Teams. This will also help you in understanding their perspective and be able to manage them in the context of a larger meeting. It is possible that you will meet them first in a group, and the same questions will apply, just in a more formal setting. For larger groups, I would recommend you prepare a presentation (see examples below) to bring focus to the meeting and keep the agenda directed. For smaller groups, a less formal approach is suitable.

Future Green Teamers: As you are learning, researching, and defining your plan, start to gain support and allies by building a peer group of like-minded staff – your future green teamers. They may be at one site or many sites. This will actually become the most important team once you start to build momentum. They will be the ones who will be your greatest source of ideas and your biggest allies to really drive behavioral change. This is also your research team for you to understand the history of the organization's green initiatives and will have the ideas on where to start. This will also be your research team. They will provide an understanding of the organizations green initiatives and ideas on how to start the process.

Implementation Plan:

After you have captured all of the feedback, you need to reassemble all of your information into a format that is consistent with the "Sustainably Green Principles" and action items. This doesn't have to be complicated. Just list out the types of things you want to accomplish. When I prepared the one for the YMCA of Greater Toronto, I felt it was important to have a team structure to demonstrate how I would build in volunteerism, define the key goals, and then create a themed strategy with a high-level schedule to create some accountability. See the example on the next page.

Presenting the Draft Implementation Plan and Vision for Support:

This is an iterative process. First you test your vision with each leader and seek their input. After the interview process, reformulate your vision, including their input. Then, present the final version to them for their approval and support. You may need to go back and forth a few times with some areas to make sure you have interpreted their input and built it into the plan. This is an engagement process that gives each group voice into the process, and also gives them a sense of pride for helping to build this plan. Some will be racing along at Mach 1, while others will require cajoling.

Once you feel the document is complete enough to present as a complete draft, I would recommend you hold a formal meeting and prepare a presentation that outlines the process you undertook, shows the final "Sustainably Green Principles", your draft Implementation Plan to seek their approval and support.

From my experience, executives in meeting will be likely to challenge your plan and the proposed steps. Keep the meeting at a strategic level – your goal is to set the rules and parameters of the organization's commitment, with future meetings to share greater detail that will also be shared. As you move into Part II of this book, you will start to demonstrate the next level of detail of how this will be implemented.

Now it's your turn to get organized!

Team Structure:

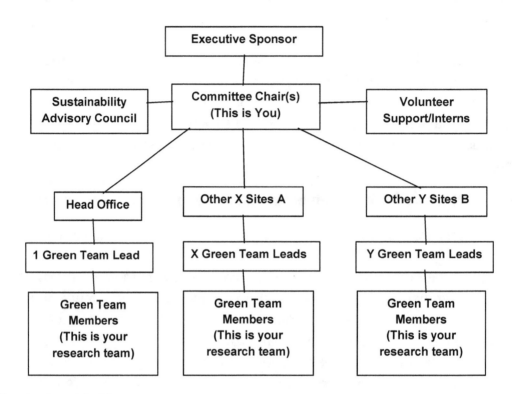

Goals for this Year:

Corporate Alignment
Draft Sustainably Green Principles
Approve with Senior Management
Update Implementation Plan

Communication Plan
Communicate Accomplishments
Staff Newsletter Update
Website Engagement

Staff Engagement
Survey Staff/Feedback
Establishing Green Teams
Events: Earth Day, Shoreline Cleanup,

Reporting
Assess Baseline Year
Develop Scorecard
Assess Comparison Year(s)

Sustainability Council
Q1 Meeting February 23rd
Q2 Meeting: June 1st
Q3 Meeting: Oct 28th
Q4 Meeting: Jan 6th

	Q1 (April – June)	Q2 (July – Sept.)	Q3 (Oct. – Dec.)	Q4 (Jan. – March)
Corporate Alignment	-Draft "Sustainably Green Principles" with senior management	-Approve "Sustainably Green Principles" with senior management	-Publish internally (along with Scorecard)	-Review annual accomplishments, set goals, update,publish -Update "Plan".
Commun-ication Plan	-Communicate accomplishments -Staff Newsletter Update	-Member communication design & rollout -Staff Newsletter piece	-Website Engagement (Intranet) -Develop comprehensive comm. plan	-Member Communication Design & Rollout Staff Newsletter piece
Staff Engagement	-Establish & Support Green Teams -Develop Green Team Toolkit & Distribute -Events: Earth Wk, Commuter Chall.	-Engage Green Teams -Events: Great Canadian Shoreline Cleanup, Speaker Series	-Engage Green Teams -Events: Speaker Series	-Engage Green Teams Events: TBD -Staff Survey -Events: Speaker Series
Reporting	-Assess Baseline Enviro Impact -Assess Comparison Yr	-Develop Scorecard (CSR-equivalent)	-Publish Internally	-Assess Comparison Year
Sustain-ability Council	Q1 Meeting: Communication Strategy	Q2 Meeting:	Q3 Meeting:	Q4 Meeting:
Operational Initiatives	-Capital Initiatives (Green) -Green Procurement	-Capital Initiatives (Green) -Green Procurement	-Capital Initiatives (Green) -Green Procurement	-Capital Initiatives (Green) -Green Procurement

Action Items:

1.   First, think about your points of inspiration: **Where did you develop your love for nature and the planet? Was it picnics on the side of the lake with your grandmother? Walks in the park with your father who commented on every moving or living thing? Overnight camp where you learned to fend off the bugs while pitching your tent, and then realized you had never felt a deeper sense of calm and peace?**

Find your inspiration, then write it down, send a note, tweet it out, pick up the phone. Talk to someone who was there or might also remember. Add some oxygen to those embers of inspiration. As you start to talk to your friends and family, you will hear other stories that will stoke the flames of passion. You will use this passion as you speak with people in your organization, you can talk about your experience and help them find their stories. Stories are what give color to our conversations - use your stories to build your green team.

 Tweet your inspirational memory: @givinggreen "inspiration"

2.   Figure out your organization. **Build a list, identify key people, and then start talking with them. This is a conversation, keep it light and interactive. Be sure to capture their ideas and test other ideas. Share the "Sustainably Green Principles" document and seek further feedback. Figure out who will support this effort to become more sustainable, those that will require more effort to convince, and those you will need to work around.**

3.   Assemble a list of your core team: **those that will become the braintrust and your initial Green Team (read more in Chapter 6, Building a Leadership and Support Team). As you start to put together your Implementation Plan and evolve your "Sustainably Green Principles" to include the feedback, start to think about how you can grow a culture of green.**

Think about the best way to introduce a structure that makes sense for your organization, but doesn't require excessive administration. Do you set up a traditional model with a Greet Team at each site? Can you leverage some existing structure? For example: we found

there was a network of staff that met about international affairs that were already discussing some of these same topics. Can you build this in a way so that people at all levels within the organization can be involved and community engagement is also facilitated. As well, the momentum will come from external sources, so think about this structure so you can delegate work and maximize participation. You don't want to try to push this alone. Remember this is built on a participatory process.

On the flip side, once you get to a point that makes sense, move ahead. You can always make adjustments or change it later to better suit future needs.

4. Use the Implementation Plan template to capture your thoughts and be able to share these ideas with others. Present this information back to your Executive Sponsor. www.GivingCharitiesGreen.com/Resources

Long shots do come in and hard work, dedication and perseverance will overcome almost any prejudice and open almost any door.
   - John H. Johnson

Never doubt that a small, close group if thoughtful, committed citizens can change the world, it is the only thing that ever has.
   - Margaret Mead, Cultural Anthropologist

Chapter 6 - Building a Leadership & Support Team

Every good leader needs a support team; a group of like-minded people who want to strive towards a deeper shade of green. I am a believer of "go big or go home." Don't limit your chances of success by your lack of creativity – think big. Jim Collins, in his book "Good to Great", talks about leadership and how to build a team. He says "First figure out your partners, then figure out what ideas to pursue. The most important thing isn't the market you target, the product you develop or the financing, but the founding team." I not sure that Jerry Maguire applied these principles the way that Jim Collins intended, but he did manage to get Renee Zellweger and a cool kid.

> **Good to Great for NFPs:**
>
> *Many people don't realize that Jim Collins also wrote a companion book "Good to Great and the Social Sectors," which he describes as "A Monograph to Accompany Good to Great." While "Good to Great" has become a standard for business success across all sectors, the short monograph is a light re-articulation of his ideas for the social sector. A great read.*

There are four levels to a leadership team that you will want to think about as you start to plan your organization's transformation:

1.   **Green Teams:** Your peer group of like-minded staff.

2.   **Executive Sponsor** (e.g. CEO, CFO, VP, Executive Director.)

3.   **Volunteer Support/Interns:** External volunteers and Interns who support you as you work to grow this strategy – your army.

4.   **Sustainability Advisory Council**: Professionals in the Environmental Sustainability field who are senior volunteers to advise you on your strategy.

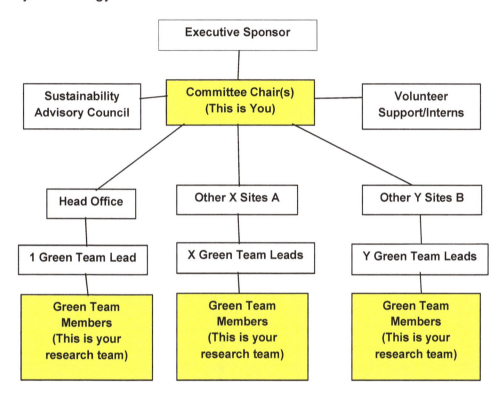

The formation of this leadership and support team usually occurs in a few steps. Here is the organizational structure that is part of the Implementation Plan. You need to alter this to suit your organization and fill it out as you move through the different stages of change. I highlighted the first group you need to think about as you prepare to become your change manager.

1.   **Green Teams:** This group consists of staff, volunteers and members/clients who are passionate about going green. The philosophy behind building Green Teams is that a commitment to sustainability must come from the top but ideas and solutions come from all the diverse areas throughout your organization. By having a green team at every location, ideas for sustainability can be generated across your organization's areas of influence. Your role and responsibility will be to facilitate communication between the Green Teams to bring a consistent approach and remain in alignment with the executive team.

The leaders from each team will form a central green "braintrust" that will act as your internal advisors for the organization. Leader representation should be obtained from all levels, and I encourage middle management or up-and-comers to be nominated as leaders. It gives them a chance to prove themselves with something they can sink their teeth into and make a difference. It is a great way to give opportunity to the future leaders of the organization.

These green team leaders will function to foster and communicate the main principles of the green initiatives and strategy to their team members at the various locations and to give voice to everyone's ideas.

Each charity will form their Green Teams to suit their organization. There is no wrong way. I recommend that each team have co-chairs – one staff person and one member or community volunteer. It helps to marry the internal mission and workings with the external perspective; as well, it helps to share the work and cover off busy schedules.

In my experience, it is easiest to start with a small staff team of keen volunteers, if possible. As the group forms and matures, I have found the most creative, comprehensive and productive teams have a majority of external volunteers. As each project or initiative is completed, celebrating the small and big successes keeps a great momentum, rejuvenates people from all of their hard work and starts to build a spirit that is infectious. Staff leaders are gaining great profile that helps to propel their "day jobs," not shirking their duties, with each success.

2. Executive Sponsor: The second-most important variable to success, after having a passionate leader to drive change, is to have executive support. This is a crucial step to the process. You need to study your executive team, understand their drivers, know who drives

> **_Why people volunteer:_**
> _In 2007, 46% or 12.5 Million people volunteered (age 15 and over) a total of 2.1 billion hours. When asked why people did not volunteer more or at all, "over half reported they were unable to make a long term commitment" or "because they were not asked."_
>
> _Other barriers included not knowing how to become involved and the financial cost associated with volunteering. (footnote: 2007 Canada Survey of Giving, Volunteering and Participating)_

change, resists it, and who will be there to back you up when you start to bring creative solutions that will challenge currents norms.

You want that person to be open, supportive, and to mentor you through the political meanderings of your organization. That person will be your contact as you evolve your plan, your business case evaluator and the key to your executive team support.

Pick this person carefully if you can – they need to be clear-headed, logical, and not swayed by politics. They need to have passion and you need to help them build trust in you and to ultimately support you.

3. **Volunteer Support/Interns:** This is your core support team. As you start to develop documentation, start tracking your environmental footprint and working on your communications strategy - this group will help to balance the load. There are so many students and recent graduates who are hungry to make an impact and gain experience working with an organization that is making green initiatives that you won't have to look hard. As long as you treat volunteers with respect, provide them with clear goals, deliverables and share the excitement, you will have no problem finding help. Interns will volunteer, or if you have a program to pay them – even better! My first two interns were paid for by the federal government as part of the recent stimulus package. These interns literally built the documentation that defined our principles, established our baseline environmental footprint, created tons of content for our marketing initiatives, and led green activities. Some of the interns have gone onto full-time positions in the sustainability sector and appreciated the learning, support, resume experience and interview references.

4. **Sustainability Advisory Council:** Developing an advisory group of experienced individuals in the sustainability industry will help to give community-minded professionals an opportunity to volunteer their time and live their ideals through a charity or NFP in their neighborhood. I have found that 80% of the people who work in the sustainability industry are doing it because they are passionate about it and truly believe in their work.

Those are the people you want to bring together to help your organization understand the external environment and provide feedback on the specific principles, goals and initiatives you are planning. For those who work in the corporate sector, you will also find these are typically the people who are connected to the foundations and charity review committees, so their knowledge of what you are doing will further your interests as you start to fundraise.

As this group forms into a high-functioning committee, they will also act as a source of credibility when you are seeking support, both internally and externally. Refer to **Chapter 7 – Getting the People Power You Need** for a discussion about recruiting and running a successful Sustainability Advisory Council. I have found this has become a place that people want to be part of – seeking ways to gain membership.

Each of these four teams will have different activities and support the implementation plan in different ways. As you start to build a list different activities and tasks, try to use these to invite someone to one of these teams to start working on something tangible that is needed now. People in each of these roles want to have impact and knowing that it fits together into a larger, well thought-out plan will help to motivate them to spend their time on your work.

Action Items:

1.   Research and build a list to seek professional advisory support. Which companies that you are already working with have departments that focus on Environmental Sustainability? Where do they meet? Find the hot spots and be there.

2.   Look around and listen carefully. Future Green Team members are distributed throughout your organization – staff, volunteers, members. Build a list of people that you want to be part of this movement.

3.   Start asking friends, peers, and family if there are students who want to volunteer some time to help you get organized in taking your organization green. Talk to schools, teachers, professors and search online sites.

Problems, as a rule, solve themselves or disappear if you remove yourself as an information bottleneck and empower others.
- Timothy Ferris, *Four Hour Work Week*

I not only use all the brains that I have, but all that I can borrow.
- Woodrow Wilson

Chapter 7 – Getting the People Power You Need

Did you know that Habitat for Humanity builds all of their homes using volunteers? Since 1976, they have built over 400,000 homes throughout the world, sheltering over two million people using only volunteers. They have volunteers that manage volunteers. What can't be done with volunteers, they hire or subcontract using donations. Do you know their trick? They are organized. They have broken down the construction of homes into a clear, concise plan.

People want to volunteer to give back to their communities in order to contribute their time or talents, but not disrupt their lives. Every volunteer experience is a combination of the individual giving and getting, not just giving. Going into a volunteering experience, people derive a lot of personal satisfaction by helping and want to feel that they are having an impact. What they often don't realize is that they get a lot more than they bargain for. They might meet another like-minded person who becomes their best friend, they might find a future employer or employee, or they might hear a story or witness a situation that is life-altering. They might even quit their job and decide that their talents are best suited to help achieve their favorite charity's mission. I have witnessed all of these happen and it gives me goosebumps!

 tweet @givinggreen "volunteer" if you've had an impactful volunteer experience.

As you develop your volunteer program as it relates to green projects, you need to ensure that people come away with some understanding of their impact on greening the environment. Remember, getting your community to reduce their environmental footprint by changing their habits and how they see the world and to drive behavioral change is your goal. **If everyone understood how every decision they made impacted the environment, and had the knowledge to make the right choice, the world wouldn't be in such disarray.**

Now you can blend the benefits of having volunteers give back to their community and positively impact their environment, while helping to advance your organization's mission – pretty cool stuff. Your volunteer program needs to be designed to extract the knowledge and experience of its members for the maximum benefit of your charity. Their diversity of experience will bring different skills, solutions and networks. The best way to reach the greatest breadth of people is to cover all cross-sections of ages, cultures, professions, backgrounds, and the many other dimensions of diversity. Volunteers will provide this cross-section of society and provide the resources that you need at low to no cost.

As you start to build a plan, you need to remember that you are already a busy person, and you have to grow your resource plan in a way that will relies on volunteers to leverage your time. Be ready to delegate without micromanaging.

Here are some examples of tasks that I have allocated to volunteers as we have built out our resource plan:

1.   A new immigrant who needed Canadian experience in the construction industry wanted to volunteer while she looked for a job. She provided an inventory of every toilet, urinal, shower and light fixture in each room of our largest building. She took pictures of the fixtures so we had them documented. We used this information to determine how much water and electricity we could save with quotes for higher efficiency fixtures. We used these quotes and the inventory to seek grant money from the local municipality and were able to save 10% of the construction cost and reduce our consumption – all made possible by the work this volunteer performed.

2.   We worked with a local university students to determine whether we could use all of the organic waste that we produce, compost it and create an organic farm to provide fresh food to our service kitchens and employment training programs. As part of the "consulting" portion of their masters program, they did a complete research assessment and feasibility plan that included waste containers, trucking, selecting composting technology and even helping to select the vegetables we should grow. There was no cost for their time and we built the organic farm in 2012, and are working on a composting program.

3.   A friend of a staff member who is very efficient at working with computers volunteered to develop a shared resource area to allow our Green Teams to share ideas and work together in a common space. It complies with our IT requirements and acts as an intranet for the Green Teams. He also took meeting minutes for us at the Sustainability Advisory Council meetings and loves to be a "fly on the wall" in meetings with these incredible executives.

4.   We had multiple volunteers come in and help us to organize our utility bills into spreadsheets so we could determine our baseline utility consumption and compare them to future years.

5.   As you can imagine, the list goes on and on as different portions of the plan start to unfold. These types of tasks will form a workplan that you can use in organizing and maximizing the help provided by volunteers and interns. Each organization tends to have their own approach for how they advertise, track, train, support and recognize their volunteers. Learn how your organization works so you can use this invaluable resource.

Tweet your green activity idea that a volunteer can do

 @givinggreen "volunteer task"

Sustainability Advisory Council: How to recruit and keep senior volunteers

Once you have completed your internal research and started to formulate the plan for how your organization will become Sustainably Green, you need to get external support to vet your plan and evolve your strategy. A Sustainability Advisory Council has three purposes:

1.   **The Support of Knowledgeable and Experienced Professionals** that will help you build a strategy and provide credibility to your organizations' sustainability initiative.

2.   **Access to Well-Placed Corporate Professionals** who have a network to assist with fund-raising and corporate partnerships. These individuals usually sit on committees that place donations. This does not mean that this council will be donating money, but helping to facilitate and create access to potential funds and foundations.

3.   **Creation of a Network of Sustainability Professionals** who will learn from each other and create their own connections between themselves. This creates an opportunity for you to be a fly on the wall as they build relationships and share best practices.

I have a few simple principles for managing volunteers:

- **Maximize the volunteers' time to be productive in the task or event you are asking them to be involved in.**

- **Respect their time by sticking to the schedule you set – end on time! If you need more assistance, arrange a future volunteer time.**

- **Ask them how it went, what could be improved and ensure they felt like they made a contribution.**

- **Thank them. Be positive, you want them to come back!**

This is crucial to keeping high-level volunteers. Do not ask them to do required homework, use their precious time wisely – they are likely working 60+ hour weeks and have families. They want to contribute to a local charity or NFP to give back in a meaningful way using their knowledge – they don't need a second job.

As you start to build a Sustainability Advisory Council, you need to have a clear plan for what you are asking of the members. Do you want their feedback on something? Do you want their opinions on next steps? Do you want them to share their successes and failures? Do you want them to share their resources? Would you like them to review something?

Always think: How will these volunteers be experiencing this? Would I like that?

They should be able to walk into a room with their peers, be greeted, thanked for giving their time, and then given an opportunity to offer their valuable knowledge and experience. They should leave the meeting feeling appreciated for the contribution they made, and have a clear understanding of their next engagement.

Hosting the meeting: When setting up a meeting agenda stick with the "KISS" approach – "Keep It Simple, Stupid." Mornings seem to work best with corporate volunteers – 90 minutes max. Keep the agenda brief and focus on one meaningful concept or task. Something that they can discuss off the top of their heads and offer opinions and recommendations.

Size of the Council: This depends on your preference, experience and how quickly you are able to move. For the YMCA of Greater Toronto, we charted a fast course and started with 12 members. Normally, I would recommend 3 to 5 key people to help polish up the policies and strategy. As you start to network with different organizations, it is nice to have capacity to offer a seat at the Sustainability Advisory Council as an element to a strategic partnership between your organization and a corporate donor. Most organizations want to engage both financially and through volunteerism, so this is something to consider.

When you are deciding which industries to include be as broad as possible. Don't fret over putting competitors together, it will make the conversation more lively. I tested this theory at my wedding (see Competition and Goodwill inset).

Day of the Meeting: Be organized, prepared and punctual. For the presentation, I recommend you have five slides or pages, and no more than eight.

- One slide that defines the agenda and to have each member talk about one or two things they are currently working on within their organization

- One slide to recap what has happened on a strategic level in your organization since the last meeting with one or two cool highlights

> ***Competition and Goodwill:***
> *Most people are surprised how competitors can work together when they are working towards a shared goal. I tested this theory at my wedding, of all places. I was laden with the responsibility of arranging the seating plan and was particularly challenged with the fact that both sets of parents had divorced and remarried. After hours of trying to position everyone in "safe" spaces, I threw my hands (and the cards) in the air and declared: they made their choices – they can all sit together. A perfect table of 8. Wouldn't you believe they had an incredible time, stood up and sang to the head table 4 times and had a merry ole time. Keeping their kids happy on their day was their shared goal.*

- One to three slides to present your main topic for discussion

- One closing slide to discuss next steps

Be careful not to spend _their_ time justifying what _you_ have done; show them the progress, shut up and listen. Once you build trust in a group, you will be amazed to see them brainstorm together and come up with incredible ideas that will benefit your organization.

Stick to the agenda, watch the time, and facilitate the meeting. Try to keep everyone engaged in the meeting. Did I mention not to keep them too long? Protect their time and get them on their way.

Frequency of Meetings: I have found that meeting quarterly is a reasonable frequency as it gives you time to make/show progress, and it isn't too much of a commitment from these busy professionals. Sending a preview of key documents before or after the meeting is reasonable, having a coffee with some of the members individually is a great way to keep continuity and seek additional feedback.

Follow-Up and Next Steps: After the meeting is over, it is important to give feedback, confirm the next date and establish action items, and thank them. If someone has offered to provide a contact, or meet with you to dig into something more deeply one-on-one, then follow up with a tactful reminder email that they can respond to. The easier you make it for them to be involved, the better engaged they will remain. The creation of an online presence where they can continue the conversation, such as a LinkedIn Group or Google Plus group.

Collaborating with other Charities, Universities, Colleges, and Other Like-Minded Groups in Your Community:

In the world of charities and Not-For-Profits, there are many groups that are working on similar things with the same community. While there are many people who believe that working with other charities (seen as competitors) can reduce your fundraising potential and lower your measurable impacts, I have found that the opposite is more often the case. Every time I extend an invitation to join with another group or charity, we sit down, explore our points of synergy, find some common goals, try working together on something small to establish trust and communication, and then – Poof! We take it to a new level. While there may be areas where you are competing for grants, or seeking support from similar companies or targeting the same membership groups, I have found that we are often talking to the same organizations about different topics. By working together, we are providing a better solution for our shared contacts, not competing. This has proven to be a significant resource support – we collaborate to achieve our shared goals.

In late 2010, I hired a woman that has been extremely important to the success of the YMCA's Green Strategy. Terri lives and breathes sustainability in all aspects of her life, is a high-functioning environmental leader, and a "connector" as Malcolm Gladwell defines in "Blink"...she is one of those people who "link us up with the world ... people with a special gift for bringing the world together." Malcolm's other categories of people are Maven (a person who accumulates knowledge and has information on a lot of different areas) and Salesman (someone with the skills to persuade us when we are unconvinced). I am a cross between a "Maven" and a "Salesman" as I love acquiring and assimilating knowledge, then developing a sales strategy and negotiating to eventual success. I am not a "connector", but once I added one to my team, we've been an unstoppable combination. You should too.

As our collaborations with our NFP and charity partners started to evolve, we built Memorandums of Understanding (MOUs) that we started to align our organization with these strategic partners. While we might not be getting money, but we are getting other benefits that include: improved credibility, in-kind services, access to volunteers, access to their funders, advertising support, access to media contacts, and another knowledgeable team member in the industry.

What I often hear from eventual donors is that it was an easy sell to participate in our project once they saw the level of organizations involved in the project. My motto is a good partnership makes one plus one equal three!

Universities, Colleges, and High Schools:

Working with educational institutions offers access to extremely knowledge professors and massive amounts of cheap or free labor – I know, I am starting to sound like a child-labor advocate! In reality, these kids want relevant experience in their fields of interest to help them prepare for their future careers. Finding relationships with professors and teachers that teach classes that can be aligned to your needs and provide real world experience to their students is perfect for schools as they see their contribution going back to the community at-large through a charity. For example, we have been working with Sheridan College over the last four years as our key energy auditing and planning partner.

Some examples of projects we have collaborated on with Sheridan College and other local education institutions include:

o Energy audits

o Energy modeling

o Indoor Air Quality (IEQ) testing

o Feasibility study for an organic farm and commercial composter

o Feasibility study on including wind and solar power to our site that included ROI evaluation and pricing details

o Studies on the impacts of green roofs

o Research papers on a multitude of topics

I especially like to bring a school to a partnership with a new technology provider as the school can provide an independent case-study, the technology provider can use the study as a marketing tool (assuming it works) and we get the technology cheaper (or free) plus get to use it as a marketing tool. See, one plus one equals three.

Environmental Charities and Foundations:

Environmentally-focused charities (Eco-Charities) often make the best partners when doing community based projects. They are often looking for projects that they can connect to their volunteers or even fund. At other times, they have existing projects that act as the perfect link with your Green Teams, lending people and expertise to assist them with their projects. It has to be a give and take to be successful.

At the YMCA of Greater Toronto, we have active partnerships with the Jane Goodall Foundation, David Suzuki Foundation, Evergreen, Earth Rangers, Earth Day Canada, World Wildlife Fund (WWF), and Terri could rattle off another dozen.

Associations:

There are complete industries that come together to standardize their craft, develop standards of care and work together to raise the bar on how their industry is perceived and accessed in the marketplace. There are tons of these associations, and include professional groups (e.g. doctors and engineers) as well as suppliers and manufacturers (e.g. concrete, flooring materials, and recycled tires.)

One of our recent partnerships was with the Ontario Tire Stewardship (OTS), an association that works with businesses that reuse recycled tires in their products and encourages them to promote their industry and find innovative ways to use their products. They partnered with the YMCA in the renewal of a facility courtyard – a space that was due for some improvements. They brought an approach that matched the YMCA's vision, a project management team, money and even managed a regional design competition with landscape and interior design students.

Other Like-Minded Charitable Organizations:

It is common to overlook organizations in your industry when looking for partners. Having spent much of my career in the For-Profit sector, competition was fierce and this type of collaboration is rare. When it comes to other charities on the ground, in your community, there are many points of synergy that can be found.

You might be competing for donors, but quite often these donors have certain motivations and your dialogue won't change that. I encourage you to reach out, be open to discussion, and look for points of synergy with these "competing" charities. Nine times out of ten, they are working with different groups on different solutions, and you can work together to do something incredible.

Every time I meet with a different charity team, I am amazed at the opportunities or lessons that I learn. Get good at having a coffee and starting a new friendship....who knows, maybe you are a connector and just needed a push.

Action Items:

1. Sample presentations are available at
    www.GivingCharitiesGreen.com

2. Educate yourself on getting and working with volunteers in
    your organization. This will become your workforce.

3. Identify possible Sustainability Council members.

    a. Large companies with which your charity has existing
        relationships.

    b. Consultants you have worked with or hired. Are there any
        recent articles in the local paper about LEED buildings?
        Look for people who are actively working on these types of
        projects.

    c. Industry associations that have a sustainability role.

4. Tweet more meeting ideas:

    @givinggreen "tips on meetings"

5. Develop a list of potential partners with Education Institutions,
    Associations, and charities. You probably are connected to
    many of these groups through you staff or existing volunteers
    and members.

6. Update your Organizational Chart to see your team form

When we refer back to the organizational structure, if you are following along, the yellow boxes should start to have some names penciled in and you are now working on the orange boxes. This is a framework, so break it apart to suit your set-up, but try to add all of these boxes. Like a good recipe, you can mix the ingredients together in different ways, but you need to include them all to get the right flavor

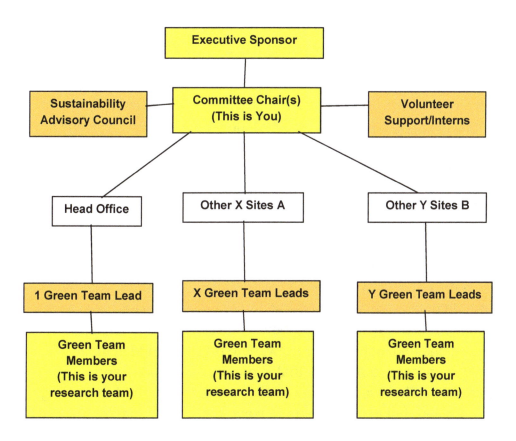

A pessimist sees the difficulty in every opportunity; an optimist sees the opportunity in every difficulty.

- Winston Churchill

You must be the change you wish to see in the world.
- Mahatma Gandhi

Chapter 8 – Getting the Grant Funding You Need

Breathing life into your organization with the dollars you need is the second reason you picked up this book (unless you are the CFO and skipped ahead to this chapter – then it is probably the first reason you picked up this book!)

This is the unique characteristic of a charity – doing what is right, and getting other people to pay for it. The fact that going green will drive money to your organization is often eye-opening – it just seems like adding more expense without a clear gain. Most charities are resource-strapped and desperately try to remain focused on their core mission and following their historical successes – they are afraid to stray too far from what they know and must constantly dodge distractions.

The concept behind this book is to translate the well-known fact that the world is on a crash course for Climactic Change, to incorporate the solution into your-day-to-day operation of running a charity, and to use this change as a way to raise money. You will give commercial organizations and individuals who want to make change in their community access to a charity that is organized, credible and inspirational. They want to work with charities that are not only doing their work well, but in a way that will leave a healed planet for future generations.

In another few years, this won't be the reason to donate to a charity… **it will be *the reason not* to donate!** Get on the band wagon while there is still some opportunity for market differentiation as this idea is starting to gain momentum. You don't want to be the organization that people choose not to donate to because you haven't kept pace with this issue.

The next two chapters work together to cover the major ways charities can seek funding. This chapter is geared towards different types of grants and "free" money that is available if you are organized. The following chapter (**Chapter 9: Getting the Corporate Funding You Need**) will describe the methodology to work with corporate partnerships and layer this into you Corporate Giving Program to attract additional funding sources.

As you review these next sections, you will find there is some additional research required to find these groups in your specific area, but this step is a necessary element for you to fund your projects – this money is there, waiting to be collected!

Grants from Governmental Agencies and Private Foundations:

There are many funding sources that businesses and homeowners access to reduce the cost of and energy-saving project. There is also a whole stream of funding sources that are available to charities that ask. Each city, town, region, municipality, state, province and federal government offers grants to encourage its constituents to reduce their consumption. They are incentivized to do this aggressively as it is considerably more expensive to create electricity, purify and pump water as well as acquire, store and distribute fuel to your home, business or institution.

Each one of these groups will offer different strategies to help its residents and businesses to reduce, and it often comes in the form of "free" money. This is not new, but the more recent strategies have made it much easier for everyone to participate.

Along-side the governmental bodies, there are Foundations from philanthropic individuals and businesses that have also established funding and a set of rules on how to access this funding.

I will not list specific sites or programs as it is quite variable by region, but I will share my experience with the common approaches and strategies.

Energy Reduction Incentive Grants for Specific Projects:

I have found that the most common and easiest approach to receive funding is based on a specific project (e.g. lighting retrofit or boiler replacement) and the grant can be accessed at any time of year. This type of grant will require you to work with a contractor or consultant. They will tell you what the current energy use is on your current technology, and they then propose a more modern and efficient technology that uses less gas or electricity.

There is typically a form that either you or the contractor can fill out to send to the government BEFORE you complete the work. Once you send the application in, wait a few weeks (sometimes longer) and they will agree to send you a check after you complete the project. The grant amount is usually a function of the amount of gas savings or electrical consumption reduction. This can be significant; especially when you are looking at very outdated lighting or inefficient heating technology.

I have presented this in a simplified format for clarity, which is often the case as you get started. You can start to replace really complex systems and will need to start working with an energy consultant to assist you with understanding your energy use in your buildings. I will cover more specific project types in **Chapter 13: Improving Your Building Systems**…at this point, the key message is to find and contact incentive programs in your area (municipal, regional and national) and seek their approval before you start replacing systems...most agencies won't offer retroactive incentives since you did the work already without their help! The other thing I always recommend is to look at the systems that are at the end of their life first...you know, that boiler that turns on and off when it wants...or the lights that always flickers. You might as well replace something old and broken first, then start to evaluate the other energy hogs in your buildings.

Water Conservation Rebates:

Municipalities incur significant costs building and running their large water treatment plants, water distribution and pumping stations and will typically offer incentives on an individual appliance level to incentivize you to buy low-flow technology. This type of rebate is typically for appliances like toilets, urinals, shower heads, faucets, etc. This varies by region, but it is typically a rebate for which you can apply for with a valid receipt or work with your installer to receive this grant.

Wastewater Reduction Grants:

Some municipalities are giving incentive grants to recognize the impact of green roofs and other systems that slow down the flow of rainwater into the municipal water systems. For instance, by adding a certain area of green roof where only concrete or asphalt existed before, the water runs more slowly into the city drains and prevents backups that flood basements or overflows that can actually contaminate regional watersheds.

In my experience, these are incentive grants that require some planning ahead of time and approval needs to be granted before you start the work to ensure you qualify. For the Green Roof project at our Central Toronto YMCA, we received almost $25,000 back from the City of Toronto. It pays!

Alternative Energy Grants and Contracts:

As you venture into the world of alternate energy, which can include solar power, wind power, and geothermal (using the soil or water in the earth for heating or cooling) and biomass technologies. There are many incentive-type grants that can be accessed. There are also contracts with regional power authorities or governments that will guarantee you a certain amount of money based on the power you create. This can work really well, but I consider this advanced and you will need to seek a consulting engineer to assist with the design. As an example, I have used this approach to put solar-thermal systems (the sun heats up the water or other fluid in tubes which is used within the building to heat our hot water) on our roof and we have had considerable success.

Carbon Credits Market:

One area that is controversial to some is the "carbon credit market". In Europe, governments require businesses to achieve a target level of carbon dioxide generation that is defined as their "carbon footprint". If they exceed their limit, they pay significant fines. This has created an equities market called "carbon trading", where businesses that generate less than their limit can sell their "carbon credits" to businesses that have a "carbon footprint" that exceed their limit for a fee. These are called "mandatory markets" where these carbon credit limits are required. In North America there exists a "voluntary market" for carbon credits where businesses voluntarily buy these carbon credits to reduce or offset their "carbon footprint." Some areas in North America are starting to flirt with the manatory markets, but the industry is young. You will sometime hear that called "carbon offsets."

Still with me? If so, you are asking: "Why would businesses want to voluntarily buy down their carbon footprint?" Great question! Many businesses see this as a marketing strategy to demonstrate they are "carbon neutral" and purchase these "carbon offsets" to achieve "carbon neutrality." So, after this long-winded explanation, this voluntary carbon market creates an opportunity for charities to generate "carbon credits" to enter this market place. For organizations that seek positive marketing, there is additional value in socially responsible carbon credits.

While this is also an advanced level funding strategy, this can be done – we did it in 2012 at the YMCA of Greater Toronto. We set up a five-year contract to sell all of the carbon credits we generate to an investment firm that re-sells them to local businesses that are trying to voluntarily become carbon neutral. These companies want to acquire credits that are created by local socially responsible organizations (like the YMCA) to demonstrate their commitment to the Triple Bottom Line (economic, social and environmental).

Some people say that we are allowing organizations to feel good about themselves by selling our credits so they can pollute more. This argument holds no water in the voluntary market – it's voluntary! I believe this practice of charities selling carbon credits will remain a worthy strategy in a mandatory carbon market as well.

At the YMCA of Greater Toronto, we made an internal decision that our goal did not have to be carbon neutrality. We have evolved our goal to: "we will sell more carbon offset credits than we consume" – meaning that we will find ways to compensate for the creation of carbon credits by becoming a net producer or carbon saver. For example, we are now exploring the possibility to offset a significant amount of carbon credits by generating electrical power using biofuel in a highly efficient generation plant; as well, to generate carbon credits created through community organic waste processing with the installation of a local vermiculture plant. These projects could create enough carbon credits to more than compensate for the carbon that is created to heat our buildings and power our lights.

One of the tricks I have learned is to keep the credits in your possession while getting all the grants you are seeking. I am constantly negotiating to keep the "environmental attributes" that allow us to use this transaction strategy of selling carbon credits.

The process of getting your carbon credits "evaluated" (quantified) and then "certified" (verified) is a timely and costly process. We were able to secure some incredible pro-bono and low-fee support to make this work. It takes time and requires good help, but can create an entirely new and exciting funding stream that breathes an additional source of cash for your business cases.

Government and Foundation Applications - Periodic:

There are numerous agencies that have annual "pools of money" that they award to successful applicants who apply to receive funding based on certain criteria that must be met. We have had considerable success receiving small grants of $5,000 to multi-million dollar grants using this approach.

This is an investment of time and energy, and you get better after doing a few, but this strategy is one that requires you to plan carefully and complete the application thoroughly. Most charities that I know are somewhat familiar with this approach as this same application process is used to secure program funding and other forms of capital grants that are not specific to environmental technology or energy reduction.

As you seek ways to build your plan that includes finding new staff or interns, this is one of the directions that you should consider. It has the greatest potential for large-dollar governmental support. Go after the small and quick grants and the large ones in parallel for the maximum effect.

Non-Government Grants:

There are many organizations that are not governmental bodies that offer grants and funding to assist charities in moving the needle towards sustainable change. As with the government grants, I will not cover specific ones as it varies so much by region. These vary based on who is providing the funding, available government grants and other agendas. The theme across all of these organizations is that they want to believe you are doing it for the right reasons, will create real impacts and that there is value for their money placed with your project or charity.

If you do your research well, you can find some amazing groups that can't find the right organizations to give their money to. One example of this at the YMCA was for a Solar-Thermal installation. The local City of Toronto provided a $76,000 grant to enable us to justify our business case for moving forward with this grant. We received further grants based on gas reductions (an incentive-based grant) from our local gas distributor as well as corporate sponsorship.

Poking your eyeball with a pencil... Are you starting to scan ahead, or worse, are you actually thinking about some form of self-induced punishment to avoid looking for these grants? If this is the type of work that makes you brain hurt, sets off your face-twitch or worse, that's okay. Not to poke your eyeball with a pencil - it is okay to understand that you need to enlist someone to help you through this part.

There are consultants available and many contractors are getting savvy enough to figure this out for you. My preference is to assign this task to a technically-inclined volunteer. Or even better, see if the consultant is willing to lend you a staff person for a period of time, or for a few hours a week to help you build this list – be creative!

Just consider the items in this chapter as **"Grant Project Funding"**. There is a lot of money available and if you did nothing else besides work on this part of the book with your facility team as a follow-up to your building assessments in **Chapter 2: Defining Your Shade of Green,** you will be your organization's hero for the amount of money you will save.

Action Items:

1.   Find a person in your organization or a volunteer to take ownership of this task. It is a great research project to find your local organizations for each of these categories. Depending on the size of your organization, you might be eligible for these grants and are missing out by not asking.

2.   Start collecting your energy bills and contact the utility companies to learn about their programs.

3.   Assemble a list of your gas, electricity, fuel and water bills tracking a list of consumption and spending by site for the last three years. You will need this for many reasons along the way – to access grants and show your future reductions.

4. Try to develop a contact with a local consulting company to support your organization.

5. Try to develop a contact with a local technical college or university to provide a place for their students to learn about energy-saving strategies and projects. You can be the "project" that they work on and gain low-cost support and advice.

6. Tweet your thoughts if you find a new grant:

 @givinggreen I love when I find "free money" from the government! We saved $2500.

We make a living by what we get, but we make a life by what we give.
  - Winston Churchill

The highest form of understanding we can achieve are laughter and human compassion.
  - Richard P. Feynman

Chapter 9 – Getting the Corporate Funding You Need

I have never been a car guy. As a kid, I loved bikes - I would find broken bikes left for garbage in our neighborhood and my dad and I would fix them up. Riding a bike was a source of freedom and gave the independence that I craved as a kid; so, once I became old enough to drive, I delayed until I was almost 19 years old. Throughout my life, cars have been a necessity - it gets me to where I'm going.

After I started my engineering business in Denver in the late 1990s, I was asked to help design the race track for the Denver Grand Prix and then oversee its installation in downtown Denver. It was extremely exciting and I thought this would be a great project to understand high-performance asphalt and maybe understand why so many people loved car races.

After an intense schedule to design, oversee the installation of the track, and to perform daily inspections on all of the temporary bridges, grandstands and platforms, (this gave me an all-access, behind the scenes pass to the event) race day was upon us. The crowds poured in, I was given a ride as a passenger around the track at Mach 1 (it was the scariest ride I've ever taken, but I suspect it will be foreshadowing to when my oldest son starts to drive.) I watched the pit crews work so furiously, the cameramen from the platforms, and the cars buzzing by. I have to admit, my love for cars didn't change – it was loud (even with the earplugs,) dirty, and smelled like oil and gas. I did take pause to witness the practiced maneuvers of the pit crews keeping the hyper-engineered cars running at top performance – they were magicians! To keep a high-performance car like this working at top condition, it requires a lot of money, talented people, exceptional coordination, and a lot of sponsorship.

When I look at the charitable sector's fundraising teams, I see it as a car that is desperately trying to stay in-motion, to minimize the repairs, to keep the tank full, and to win a race, or at least pass the finish line.

Now, some organizations are lean and mean, running an old Chevette – hopelessly trying to keep the wheels on and fuel in the tank; while others, they have BMWs that are humming along with sparkplugs properly greased and the tires sparkling. Most are somewhere in between.

So, are you are asking: What does this have to do with corporate fundraising and how does it relate to green? Another great question! This chapter is about taking your jalopy, and turning it into a hybrid, without pulling over. What this requires is an existing car – a fundraising team – to work with an existing donor-centered fundraising strategy that includes individuals, businesses and Foundations.

Building a fundraising team with a developed donor-centered strategy is bigger than this book; it is part of the fundraising industry with specialists, certifications, associations, and consultants....this is not that. What this chapter describes is the principles that were applied and some of the solutions that were used to take an existing fundraising program, and add a green theme…make it a hybrid.

In my experience and research, there are charities that focus only on environmental sustainability outcomes (e.g. Green Peace and World Wildlife Fund) and then those that focus on social, education, spiritual and health issues. I found it surprising that adding a green theme into this latter group is not widespread; in fact, there are senior consultants in the industry actively trying to talk charities out of doing this.

Many of these existing charities have incorporated some elements, (recycling, energy improvements, moving to electronic communication, etc.) but not many have made deep structural changes to how they work to include Green Fundraising at an atomic level. Each year, more and more charities are taking the risk and reaping the rewards. Like at the YMCA, they are proving that it works and moving up the bar in this industry. *Figure this out while this can still differentiate your charity!*

Understanding your Corporate Giving Program

Corporations tend to be large businesses with multiple locations, hundreds of employees and contain evolved marketing teams. These Corporations have a mandate to make money and they work with local charities to support their marketing goals (usually aligned with their target end-users). Their Human Resources (HR) teams have a mandate to attract and keep great staff; thus, most Corporations have developed a series of employee retention programs. One of these external employee retention programs is the Corporate and Social Responsibility (CSR) programs that create an opportunity for the Corporation to support their employees in community work that includes volunteering, donations and sponsorships.

The essence of the Corporate Giving Program is to create a demand to drive donations to your organization. Each charity has its own philosophy and process, but the common themes are to develop relationships with the individuals at the Corporation that are responsible for selecting a charity, and to tell a compelling story that connects the Corporation to the charity. The more successful charities develop deeper roots with the Corporations, not just with the individuals. These deeper relationships are developed by forming "Strategic Partnerships" with the Corporation and the charity to find a common theme that both organizations can work together on to meet their shared goals. When adding Green to your Corporate Giving Strategy, this is where we start.

This is really important to understand: adding Green to your fundraising program requires the people within your charity to think about how to synergize with the Corporations that will support them. You will be connecting their marketing goals and their CSR programs into a package of shared goals that simplify their work, and brings funding and resources to your charity. In simple terms, you want their money and people, and they want a great charity to place their money and people. The rest of the work is how your charity creates something that the Corporation says "We want to be a part of that!"

These synergies can be as simple as a Sponsorship for an event that allows them to associate their brand with your charity, or as complicated as an intricate volunteering program where their staff volunteer time, make regular donations and sit on each other's Boards as well as co-develop events. You are limited by your imagination.

What about individual donors, smaller businesses or Foundations, shouldn't they be considered? Yes, and they are. If you alter your fundraising process to accommodate the Corporations, the smaller businesses, individual philanthropists and Foundations will blend in seamlessly. These other groups are already built to work with charities or flexible enough to change. Corporations are more rigid and thus more challenging to work with.

Adding Green to your Corporate Giving Strategy:

When adding green to the existing Corporate Giving Program, there are three key themes that have emerged as really important to its success:

1. Establishing Credibility that your Organization is "Going Green": By building your Sustainably Green Principles document, you are creating a clear mandate and plan for taking your organization green. This is the start of your charity establishing credibility to be on the path to become "Sustainably Green" in the marketplace. I cannot stress enough that this has to be a conscious and committed decision to become environmentally responsible, not a charitable equivalent to green-washing. The key elements to build this credibility are:

o Establishing Green Teams or some form of front-line empowered group that will act as the main connection point for future projects and ideas.

o Establishing a Sustainability Advisory Council will amp this up to another level as it will marry the external perspective on green with a strong corporate connection as discussed in **Chapter 5: Getting Your Organization Organized**. The fundraising team was a permanent part of this council and helped to set it up.

o Developing an Environmental Scorecard that identifies your organization's imprint on the planet and your plan to change it. In **Chapter 10: Building Your Green Fund**, I will cover the strategy that worked for the Y.

o Working with the media to create visibility by getting published, interviewed, and included in studies, as well as using social media.

○ Applying for awards and recognition that will further enhance this credibility. I cover some of the strategies we used at the YMCA in **Chapter 16 – Getting Connected and Communicating Your Work**.

Your credibility will become the basis for your ability to raise funds with individuals, corporations and Foundations. Treat this carefully, professionally and remain transparent in your decisions, and it will grow with your successes.

2. Developing Projects that Include Volunteerism: We don't encounter enough risk takers in life, but as you start to speak with the individuals that run the Corporate and Social Responsibility (CSR) departments, you quickly realize that this group consists of risk takers, people who challenge the norm and are willing to fight for what they believe in. As you develop projects in your buildings and in your communities you will be designing them in a way to include these CSR teams. This is your charities "in" to the company if the other approaches do not work. CSR teams struggle to find local and relevant volunteer projects. If you can paint a picture that demonstrates your charity is an organization that is moving to be Sustainably Green while continuing to do the necessary social, spiritual and/or health-related work in your shared community, and then create individual volunteer experiences that supports this, you will be successful. Your goal is the:

Creation of meaningful community engagement projects that includes opportunities for volunteerism that allows employees to get out of their buildings and into the community to meet their social and sustainability objectives.

As you assess your organization's impact on the environment (**Chapter 2: Defining Your Shade of Green**), you will build a list of solutions and projects. The second half of this book (**Part II: ACTION!**) there are a series of detailed chapters that describe how to find, develop and implement these types of projects in a way that incites passion and inspires your community. As you start to get really good at developing these projects and working with your community, you will find that some of your corporate partners will offer the volunteer labor from their organization for what they can do, and then send you a check for the balance.

3. Creation of a Green Fund: This fund is to receive donations that will support your organization's green initiatives and something that could be made part of your charity's donor-centered giving strategy. For many organizations, traditional giving is directed to operational needs, to capital projects, or to an endowment fund. The endowment allows us to use the interest and keep the principal for future years and is a gift that keeps giving. This "Green Fund" concept rethinks this endowment approach as follows:

a. Your charity builds a suite of initiatives that will meet your key environmental goals.

b. Organizations and individuals who give to this fund will be helping to fund projects that will create annual operational savings immediately.

c. The operational savings are captured and redirected to assist your existing programming AND be will be helping you reach your environmental goals.

d. As you pull all of your projects together into a "suite of initiatives" or portfolio of projects, you are organizing in a way that clearly defines your sustainability goals in actual metrics.

In **Chapter 10: Building Your Green Fund**, I will take you through a light business case exercise that helps you start to construct a Green Fund, explore how we evaluate and apply the metrics, and incorporate the incentive-based funding to calculate your initial return that I prefer to present as "payback years", or the time to recoup your initial capital investment. Just as I asked you to think about the funding options presented in **Chapter 8: Getting the Grant Funding You Need** as the first part of your funding - **Grant Project Funding,** the items discussed thus far become **"Donation Project Funding."** You need both project funding parts for your most successful projects!

Building your Hybrid:

The fundraising team's process is often the sacred cow in a charity. There is a fear that changing anything will tip the balance and coming crashing down. If there is concern that altering your process by adding a hybrid will be too significant for your organization, then you need to stop and look around. The world of fundraising is changing fast with the changes in how we gather information, find prospects and gain funding. As you explore adding a hybrid engine to your fundraising car, you need to be looking at the car's console as well – Do you use social media effectively (rebuild your car radio)? Do you have a good website (add a GPS system on the console)? Are you getting recognized or noticed for your work (stickers on the car)? These changes can start small to build momentum, but keep the key themes in-mind to allow this to grow and upgrade your jalopy into a car that will last for many more races!

Action Items:

1.   Find the key person in your organization that leads the fundraising or fund development strategy and have them read this chapter. They should read the whole book, but this chapter is a good place to start to whet their philanthropic appetite.

2.   Find the key person in your organization who handles volunteering and have a conversation around the types of projects people are asking for, the top 10 organizations that you are working with and how often. Make a list of the top 3 companies that have a fit with environmental sustainability goals as part of their CSR platform and community outreach goals.

3.   Bring these top 3 companies to the fundraising team and start the discussion around building a deeper alliance with this organization. Try to facilitate a discussion with these companies to see if you can build on some recent successes to work towards a project that gets them volunteering and donating.

4.   Tweet your thoughts:

> **@givinggreen My charity is committed to "green fundraising"**

 or

> **@givinggreen we had 20 people and $5000 from ABC Corporate rebuild our playground with "green fundraising"!**

Fundraising is the gentle art of teaching the joy of giving.
  - Hank Rosso

The greatest use of a life is to spend it on something that will outlast it.
  - William James

Chapter 10 – Building Your Green Fund

I didn't realize that I was a list person until about five years ago. Every time my wife and I would take our two boys to visit my brother-in-law's family for three or four days, he would send me a list of things he was hoping I could "help him" with around the house. I would glance through the list, pack the appropriate tool boxes in advance and we would drive to Ottawa to get our two families together.

We would skate on the canal, eat our Beaver Tails (if you don't know what those are, you need to go there and find out!) and then head back to their house. Over a few days I would manage to fit in all of his tasks – and these weren't small tasks. One time I drywalled their entire garage (…because my niece's room above it got cold in the winter); another, I installed crown molding, a chair rail, replaced their kitchen faucet and temporarily patched their leaking roof.

One evening, my wife wondered aloud how I manage to get all of his stuff done in Ottawa while the stuff at home remains partially completed. My brother-in-law remarked "Alex can't leave a list undone. He likes lists. I buy the supplies and send a list and it gets done." So, as it turns out, I like lists.

The concept of the Green Fund is simple: it is a list, but it often requires hard work to keep it simple for others to understand. Oh, and once we make the list, we have a goal and become tenacious to complete the list.

This chapter will give you the tactics as well as the deeper technical strategies to create this fund. It can be as formal as is sensible for your organization and available resources. The essence of this Green Fund is to allow partner organizations and individuals to donate to your charity in a way that will help you serve your community better, reduce your environmental impact and meet their philanthropic goals. All while educating the community on how to reduce their environmental impact.

As a reminder from **Chapter 1: The Concept and Why This Works**:

This "Green Fund" concept flips the endowment approach on its head and works as follows:

Your charity builds a suite of initiatives that will meet your key environmental goals. People who give to this will be helping to fund projects that will create annual operational savings immediately. The operational savings are captured and redirected to assist your existing programming AND will help you reach your environmental goals.

What does the donor get?

> They meet their philanthropic goals to donate
> towards a project or fund in a charity they believe in
> +
> They are improving the health of the environment
> in their own community or near the areas they operate
> +
> The savings from their gift continue to fund the charity year after year.

When building this "Fund", the concept borrows on the idea of a high quality mutual fund (think: Green Fund) where a portfolio manager purchases a bunch of stocks (environmentally-focused projects) that require an investment (donation of money and volunteer hours) and will create a financial return (reduced carbon footprint, operational expense savings, tax receipt.)

The "Fund Manager" has a mandate, or set of principles (Sustainably Green Principles) that defines how they select their stocks (green projects) and they track their investment metrics (financial savings, energy reduction, carbon footprint reduction, volunteer hours, etc.)

You want to report on the overall impact of the fund while keeping track of the specific projects contained within the portfolio. The analogy is loose and I carry it only to the level presented here to help you understand it and explain it to other financial-minded people. There is a simplicity to the model that people understand and it becomes another segment of your charities overall donor-centered giving plan.

In order to prioritize projects that will be easier to fundraise, you can divide the projects into "designated" (i.e. those that sponsors will find attractive and fund directly) and "undesignated" (i.e. projects that make business sense and move the needle towards your green objectives, but aren't really attractive to funders.) When there is a choice, I encourage people to keep their donations "undesignated" to create maximum flexibility.

For the YMCA of Greater Toronto, we created three main metrics that we seek to impact when developing a project:

1. Air Quality

   A. Electrical Reduction (kW-hrs)

   B. Fuel/Gas Reduction (cubic meters, cubic feet or gallons)

   C. Greenhouse Gas (GHG) Reduction (metric tons of CO_2e per year)

2. Water Reduction (gallons or cubic liters)

3. Greenspace Restored (acres or square feet)

To keep the discussion simple, we further consolidate items #1 and #2 to "Energy Savings" in equivalent gigajoules per year (GJ/yr). As we externally share the impacts of our projects, we boil these down to Air Quality (metric tonnes of CO_2 equivalent or CO_2e per year), Water (cubic meters or gallons) and Land (acres or square-feet) as this is easier for people to metabolize.

Still with me? Having flashbacks to science class that you thought you had already passed? As with the investment "mutual fund", having someone look at the technical side of the "portfolio" gives credibility to funders that give both grants and donations.

Build your team with people that aren't afraid to dig into this level of detail. You know when Al Gore talks about the Global Climatic Change, it is this information he is referring to: tonnes of Greenhouse gases, kW of electricity, GJ of energy. For the YMCA of Greater Toronto, we followed this strategy and then requested contractors and consultants to provide their projects in this format, so they did the hard work and we just had to organize it. For complex projects, consultants were hired to work on this, for simpler ones, I did it.

Here is an example: we were interested to see the impact of a solar thermal array (solar hot water system we put on our roof). Therefore, I asked for the following metrics:

- Capital Cost ($)
- Annual Savings ($)
- Annual Maintenance, and typical years for upgrades ($)
- Life of the Installation (years)
- Metric Tonnes of Carbon reduced per year (CO_2e/yr)
- Volume of Natural Gas reduced per year (m^3/yr or ft^3/yr)
- KiloWatt-hours of electricity saved per year for each year over its life (kW-hr)
- Equivalent GigaJoules saved per year over the expected life (GJ/yr)
- Available grants that would reduce the capital installation ($)
- Number of Years to Payback the Initial Capital Investment (years)
- Type of monitoring or control system to measure the impact

In addition to the technical information related to the actual project, I would also capture the volunteer hours, number of volunteers and total donations received.

Gathering, developing and updating this information is the perfect type of project for a technical volunteer. At the YMCA of Greater Toronto, we ended up working with a local technical college that organized all of this information, assessed our full environmental impact, and assisted us to actually sell our carbon offset to a carbon fund manager that resells our carbon offsets to corporations that are trying to become carbon neutral.

How you define the parameters of your "Green Fund" is up to you. Initially, we looked for rapid payback in facility-related projects to build some momentum on lighting retrofits, moving to higher efficiency heating systems, etc. We then grew to bigger projects.

My brain is throbbing....OK, I can feel your brain is starting to ache...this is too hard, I never want to know what a GigaJoule is!! Let's start small. Get up from your chair or hammock and look around the building. We will make a list of a few things that are in the room you are in right now to build your confidence, ready? Get up, stretch, touch your toes, do a little wiggle and find a lightbulb.

Seriously, find a lightbulb. I want you to find one in a lamp, in a pot-light ceiling fixture and figure out if it's a CFL (screw-shaped) or the old-style incandescent. Maybe it is an LED with lots of smaller lights inside. Look further to find a fluorescent bulb. Is the bulb the size of a paper towel roll? If so that is a T-12, they stopped manufacturing those bulbs in 2010!

If you replaced that bulb right now, the money you save in electrical costs will pay for the work after 12 to 16 months. Look further – find an emergency exit sign. Is there a white light shining out of the bottom? Can you peer inside and see an incandescent light? These are always on...this one also pays for the cost to replace it with electrical savings in about a year. After that, you are just spending less on each electrical bill.

Example exercise:

This little exercise will help to demonstrate a very obvious problem and a solution that is likely sitting in your house or office....or cabana if you are enjoying this on the beach... "A word problem!" you shout in disgust – it's OK, you can let me do the work on this one, this is REALLY IMPORTANT TO UNDERSTAND.

Back to our light bulb field trip. Let's assume you found one incandescent bulb – sorry, I imagine your eyes are still burning from staring at that bare bulb! Let's also say your 100 Watt bulb is on for half of the hours in a week and that costs $1 to replace each bulb. If you pay 12 cents per kilowatt-hour*, you are spending about $4.40 per month in* electricity to use that one bulb for 12 hours a day. If you were to replace that bulb with a CFL (at a cost around $3) you would pay 75% less electricity or about $1.10 per month.

The average price was **12¢/kWh** in the U.S. in mid-2012 for residential electricity, and ranged from **8¢** to **36¢** - reference DoE; for Canada, the average in mid-2012 was **11¢,** and ranged from **7¢ to 15¢** - reference MB Power

So, if you had a $5 bill in your hand, you could use most of it to pay the electrical bill ($4.40 per month) or buy a CFL for about $3, and then each month you will be saving more than $3. If only all of your financial decisions were this easy. Your payback period is about one month. What I didn't tell you is the CFL lasts more than 10 times longer on average and looks really cool with the spiral shape (as if you didn't already notice!)

This is important for two reasons:

1 – This demonstrates how an investment today for $3, plus the time buying and installing it will benefit you each and every month. This is the essence of the first phase of setting up your Green Fund. Find examples that save you money and meet your goals for reducing your impact.

2 – Step back and think about how easy that example was to figure out. You walked around your house, your business or your local coffee shop (your cabana?) and learned how to save $3 each month for one bulb, or $30 each month for 10 bulbs! Now if something as simple as a replacing a light bulb - something that you can buy at the grocery store when you pick up your milk - is this readily accessible, you can imagine the opportunities for improving energy in more complicated systems that few people understand; and, the potential savings are huge! This isn't a judgment, 82% of the North American market relies on incandescent bulbs (Source: Earth 911, Info Dingo), this is the norm and why we need to take steps like this forward.

Getting Organized:

Let's use our light bulb example to track the details of the project in a spreadsheet that allows you to organize and compare projects that will start to make up your Green Fund projects.

Project Location: La Cabana (near the palm tree)
Project Name: Replace 10 light bulbs with CFLs
Installation Type: Electrical Savings
Project Cost: = $30 + 1 hour time to buy, unscrew and re- screw
Annual Savings: = 12 months x ($4.4-$1.1) x 10 bulbs =$396
Years to Payback: = $30 cost / $396 savings = 0.075 years = 0.9 months

I have an extended version of this spreadsheet located at www.GivingCharitiesGreen.com/Resources that captures the basic information that was used for years to track projects. This spreadsheet was the foundation of what was later used to sell our carbon credits, so it was successful in capturing most of what was needed. You can modify this to work for your organization, and make it as simple or complicated as you need. As you fill this spreadsheet out with more complicated projects, you will want to refer back to the **Project Funding Parts A and B.**

Now it's time to build your list.

Action Items:

1. **Download the form www.GivingCharitiesGreen.com/Resources and start building your list. One per site. One per team. Let the list-making begin! Pull together what you learn into this format and keep adding as more ideas are discovered. We will work through this list building in greater detail in Part 2: ACTION.**

2. **Buy CFLs. Walk around your house, your office and even your parents' house and replace a bunch of bulbs.**

3. **Tweet your thoughts:**

 **@givinggreen I have 10 new CFLs in my Cabana from the "Green Fund"**

We are in community each time we find a place where we belong.
- Peter F. Block

Always in motion is the future.
- Yoda

Chapter 11 – Measuring Your Environmental Footprint

Many have heard the phrase "You can't manage what you don't measure," but the optimist in me prefers Peter Drucker's quote "What's measured, improves." Your organization's environmental footprint may differ from others, but in my experience there are common themes that emerge, and then you put an emphasis that is appropriate for your organization.

For the YMCA of Greater Toronto, we highlighted water due to the fact that we own and operate many pools and use significant amounts of hot water. Some will choose to focus on carbon footprint as it's the simplest impact to measure. I believe you should strive to be broader than that, and set your measurable goals so you can focus on your priorities. As Stephen Covey says "Begin with the end in mind."

Simple is Best

Keep your message simple, people don't want to think too hard – they want to understand your impact simplistically. After many trials and tribulations, we evolved our strategy into three simple points, air, water and earth. Such a simple message seems to resonate with donors, staff and even politicians.

Initially we tried to use the structure of our Sustainably Green Principles to display our plan, but we were using internal and technical language to express our goals externally. Having an internal structure to organize your ideas, successes and plans is critical to keeping organized and remaining sufficiently scalable; however, when you start speaking with broader internal and external audiences, follow the KISS approach - Keep It Simple, Stupid. When you break it down, people understand it:

Air – the air we breathe should be fresh, not laden with chemicals and poisons that yield acid rain, smog and plumes of noxious exhaust.

Water – the source of life for all living things. We rely on clean water to drink, play, and keep a rich bio-diversity.

Earth – the planet that has given us the natural resources to run our modern civilizations. Coal and oil reserves are finite and have created significant pollution. The waste we create is buried in more and bigger landfills across our regions. The food we eat relies on nutrients, but can only feed so many. The houses and businesses are built using resources from the land, but can only sustain so many.

By 2020, the YMCA of Greater Toronto, with the help of our communities, will leave:

CLEANER AIR

33% reduction in CO_2 emissions (5,000 tons)

FRESH WATER

27% reduction in H_2O usage (92 million gallons annually)

NATURAL SPACES

Reclaim 15% of our land acreage (140 acres)

By 2040, we strive to be carbon neutral or sell more carbon offsets than we use.

Live a Little

As I delve into the technical sides of driving change, I continue to keep myself inspired by finding vacation destinations with rich bio-diversity (nature in its purest form) to build memories for my family, especially my boys, to develop an understanding and appreciation for our planet through our own eyes and experiences. You should also find ways to keep yourself inspired.

Talk a walk along the beaches on the western coast of Vancouver Island near Tofino where the sea lions, bald eagles, star fish, and grey whales in the distance are a typical activities in an adventure-day along the Pacific Coast. Jump in a sea kayak and then climb to the top of Signal Hill with hopes to witness an iceberg or a pod of humpback whales floating along the Atlantic shores of St. Johns, Newfoundland. Wander through the Desert Botanical Gardens in Phoenix, Arizona to witness the 137 different cactus species amongst an incredible desert setting with occasional humming birds darting by. Pick the sand out of your toes after skipping through the surf along the shores of Jupiter, Florida. Climb to the top of Whistler Mountain (after the stunning gondola ride) and look out over the horizon at the Rockies to notice a golden eagle circling above Lake Alta. Walk the Southern Californian rocky coast along Terranea's shores and witness pelicans fly by in perfect formation above the hundreds of feeding dolphins that swim past.

Over the time I have been writing this book, those are some of the highlights I have enjoyed. Don't forget to explore and enjoy the planet you are trying to save for future generations.

Finding your inner Investigative Reporter

As Julia Roberts did so well in her portrayal of Erin Brockovich's mission to unearth the hazardous polluting habits of Pacific Gas & Electric Company, you need to arm yourself with a clipboard and go on a fact-finding mission. On a much smaller scale than Erin (I hope!) you will seek to understand how all of the different parts of your organization affect the environment and will help to improve your organization's impact.

Gathering information to develop your environmental footprint depends on the systems, vendors, and purchasing habits of your organization.

Sometimes this is easy when purchasing is centralized, vendors are sophisticated and systems are automated and current. Usually we aren't so lucky. You will find that there is some data that you are able to access, and then you will find others scattered throughout your organization. Do not get overwhelmed – measure what you have, then start to look ahead, one step at a time.

Step 1 - Cozy up to your friendly accounts payable person or controller:

Spend some time in the Accounting or Finance Department learning what types of reports can be run. At this stage of the game, you are at the mercy of what they have already been tracking. The answer to the questions vary from ultra-complex tracking with a lot of reporting to someone entering into a simple Excel spreadsheet. Some key items to look for are energy costs (gas, oil, electrical), water costs, staff mileage, vehicle rentals, air travel, and a list of vendors.

Step 2 - Try to figure out the basics:

Buildings: Build on the inventory of locations you created when you started to track the breadth of your physical impact. List out the sites, their addresses, whether they are owned vs. leased, their square-footage, electrical consumption, gas consumption and water consumption. Determine if you have air-conditioning units, how many people work there, and how many people visit or use their services.

Supplies: Develop a list of what you buy, from whom, and how often. If you have a Procurement or Purchasing group, this will be in their files.

Transportation: List the number of vehicles you own, lease and rent. Look to see if you track mileage by capturing the total distance that staff drive for work as recorded on their expense reports. For airline travel, do you have a travel agent that tracks this information?

Step 3 - Determine Your Baseline Year:

In order to understand where you need to go, you must first understand where you are. Your baseline year is a point in time when you have a reasonable chunk of information about your organization's consumption to develop a "baseline" or starting point. Each year, you will reference your changes relative to this point in time to measure the impacts.

Finding and organizing this information is powerful, but can be a lot of work depending on the systems you have in-place.

If there is a finance system that has captured a good percentage of this information, then you should rely on that data. If it is all very manual, then this year should be your baseline year. Was there a big project last year that you want to demonstrate as an improvement? Then target the year before. The trick with this decision is you do not want this to become a make-work project. Go back as far as you can with minimal work. Fill in the gaps if you can, then calculate your environmental footprint for your baseline year.

It is important to remember that this will never be a perfect continuum of data – seriously, get that idea out of your head. You will have some data in the early years, and you will build on it each year. This happens in every organization – note the asterisks littered throughout the CSR reports that are out there.

If you can acquire your energy data (fuel and electrical), that is the vast majority of your carbon footprint, and a foundational piece of your environmental footprint. As an example for the YMCA, we selected 2008 as our baseline year. It was the first year of a new finance system and provided a consistent platform for annual reports that we used in the data collection as we moved ahead.

Step 4 – Develop Your Key Categories:

Using your Sustainably Green Principles as your guide, and the possible data that you can retrieve, put together a list of what you will be tracking. Keep a focus on the areas that your organization will have the most potential to impact. Most organizations use electricity, gas, and produce waste that should be tracked. Below is an example using the over-arching goals of Air, Water, and Earth. The asterisk (*) denotes Greenhouse Gas (GHG) or impact on the carbon footprint

- Clean Air

- Electrical Consumption (*)

- Natural Gas Consumption (*)

- Other Gas Consumption (*)

- Gasoline

- Diesel

- Heating oil

- Staff Mileage (*)

- Fleet Mileage (*)

- Commuting Impact (*)

- Refrigerant Released (*)

- Fresh Water

- Water Consumption (*)

- Natural Spaces

- Acreage of natural spaces

- New green roofs or other natural spaces that were created

- Restored forests and natural spaces

- Amount of Garbage Produces/Created (try to get your vendor to give you this data)

- Paper consumption (*)

- Printer paper

- Marketing materials

- HR reports/checks

- Business cards, letterhead, and envelopes

- Amount of Recycled Materials

- Plastics/paper from your municipality or vendor

- Batteries

- Organic Waste

Step 5 – Carbon Neutrality:

To ability to declare that your organization will be carbon neutral will depend on your organization's impact. My belief is that you need to set some goals and then figure out how to get there. As a charity, we have certain responsibilities to our donors. Personally, I do not believe that we should pay for carbon credits to offset our footprint with the resources we have. While it does have a positive impact and is a good solution for commercial businesses, charities should be on the selling side of that transaction as discussed in **Chapter 8: Getting the Grant Funding Your Need**.

I think charities should be more creative…get your expanded Green Teams involved in community cleanups and rejuvenation of green spaces, helping to educate small businesses to improve their inefficient lighting, and/or wasteful heating, work on recycling events. Again, this list is only limited by your imagination and networks. No matter how you get there, set a target, even as a target as distant as 2040, to set the direction.

Step 6 – Prepare your Environmental Scorecard:

The Environmental Scorecard will become your consolidated tracking tool to demonstrate the impact your organization has generated. While corporations have CSR reports, charities should have an Environmental Scorecard to capture and share this import information. Once this has gone through some iterations to prove it works for your organization, I recommend this be blended into your Annual Report, to further express your impact on the communities your charity serves.

Once the data has been retrieved and organized on a spreadsheet by year according to the key categories, you need to start crunching the data. If you find that this gets too technical, you should try to see if you can recruit a volunteer to pull this together.

Another good option is someone in your accounting/finance group. This is straight spreadsheet work. The first order of business is to sum up the totals for each category. The second step is to convert the items that impacts the carbon footprint, and convert them to the carbon dioxide equivalent, or CO_2e. Each item has a corresponding factor that is used in the calculation for determining CO_2e. These factors vary based on your region and change each year. As an example, the efficiency of your local electrical provider and distribution network is much more efficient in Quebec, Canada with the hydroelectric power created from dams than, say, Hawaii where it is on a remote island.

Here is an early example of an Environmental Scorecard from the YMCA of Greater Toronto:

Action Items:

1.   **Build your Plan. After spending time talking with the different groups in your organization, put together a framework for your environmental footprint.**

2.   **Identify your Baseline Year.**

3.   **Build your Scorecard. Now that you know what you have, you need to define where you want to go. Be bold and set a direction!**

4.   **Tweet your thoughts:**

 @givinggreen we defined our "environmental footprint" goals to 2020

It's the action, not the fruit of the action, that's important. You have to do the right thing. It may not be in your power, may not be in your time, that there'll be any fruit. But that doesn't mean you stop doing the right thing. You may never know what results come from your action. But if you do nothing, there will be no result.
- Mahatma Gandhi

Take time to deliberate, but when the time for action has arrived, stop thinking and go in.
- Napolean Bonaparte

A good plan, violently executed now, is better than a perfect plan next week.
- George S. Patton, US General

PART II: ACTION!

Geez...that was a lot of talking, planning, thinking...where is the action? The planning piece is important and I am a strong believer in taking time to build the plan (to a certain point,) then work the plan. It doesn't have to be perfect, but must be directional, have principles and some understanding of priorities.

The other really important part is you just took two to three steps forward with your leadership team and moved them through the stages of change:

o   **Pre-Contemplation:** when they were not really aware of the problem

o   **Contemplation:** when they kind of understood it, but weren't ready to make a move

o   **Preparation:** with them helping to build a list of things to do

o   **Action:** as they explained what they were already doing!

Congratulations! Cultural change is no small feat! This approach to consensus-based planning is an effective style to moving collective minds towards a greener planet.

Now we start to focus on action! For those of you that like charts, the chart below shows my experience at the YMCA of Greater Toronto and has been confirmed by many others in both the charitable and commercial worlds. The processes are not linear, nor in series, as these activities occur simultaneously with different amounts of effort and impact. There is a considerable amount of work involved in the first phase; hence, I have devoted half of this book to building the plan and setting up systems to monitor your impact. As you can see in this chart, you need to exert a lot of effort and focus to start the energy that will "move the flywheel" and build momentum.

In your shoes, I would be going bonkers if someone said all of this planning must happen first, then I can move into action. I was pushing action in some areas, right when I started. In fact, you might notice that your action curve is probably halfway through Phase I, and depending on your facilities team, into Phase II. If that is the case, you need to get hopping!

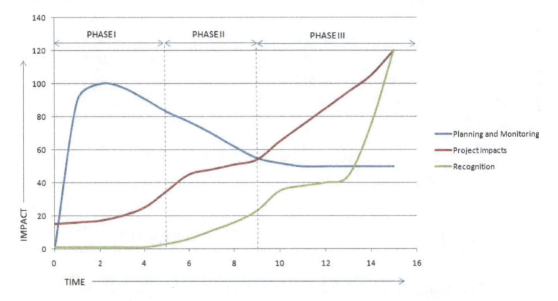

Identifying your organization's "project impacts" can be as simple as finding all of the existing successes within it and building a stronger support system for the group responsible. As you identify those early successes, you will want to build on them with more quick wins, finding ways of winning over the non-believers; as well as, driving down your consumption and wasted spending by taking advantage of the opportunities in the marketplace for reducing your consumption and carbon footprint.

As momentum starts to build, recognition will start to occur. If you are planful about the goals of your organization, and build the support systems to continue this progression, you can drive this momentum to transform your organization and have major impact! Get excited – this is where you start to see changes happen!

"**PART I: Look Before You Leap**" breaks down much of the Planning and Monitoring Curve and you can see that this phase requires a lot of up-front work. The next few chapters will break down the Project Impacts curve into three phases:

> PHASE I: Building Momentum (Green Teams)
> PHASE II: Reducing Your Carbon Footprint (Facilities Team)
> PHASE III: Inspiring Changes in your Community (Everyone)

The final chapters will discuss Marketing and Communications, Recognition, and Celebration.

Simply being with other people who are also seekers and who are involved in the same quest you are is very meaningful.
- Dan Wakefield

Happiness is not so much in having as sharing.
- Norman MacEwan

Chapter 12 – Building Momentum with Green Teams

There are many small changes that can be made that improve the imprint your charity leaves on the world. These changes are often quite minor, but require some understanding about the specific issues and operations of the organization.

For most charities, this is the type of work you are already doing: solving problems, connecting people in need with solutions based on your knowledge or awareness. When it comes to a lot of the changes that need to happen related to sustainability, we just need to get these problem solvers a new set of solutions. And the best part is that many people have these solutions, they just don't feel empowered to implement them.

As you think about a Green Team, consider it a group of staff and volunteers who want to do the right thing. They have a lot of ideas about how to work more efficiently and a will to make a change – often in a way that is educational to your organization as well as the community in general.

What they often lack is access to people within your organization who understand your needs and objectives. They don't want to disrupt the great work that you are doing, but want to help you do it even better. They just don't know where to plug in. Once you have developed your organization's principles, your next step is to open lines of communication to gain access to the unharnessed resources who want to help you implement your plan. It underlines the importance of transparency.

Advertise your vision, objectives, goals and successes. You have no idea who might be able to help you get there.

During the completion of the activities in the first part of this book, you will have had discussions with key staff at all levels of your organization and you will now have a sense of those individuals that are gung-ho and ready to come together. You have spoken to people who use your charity's services or access your programs to give some external perspective on the changes that need to happen (e.g. add recycling and change your old lights.) You might have even put together a list of potential Green Team members. Well, now is the time to start bringing them all together.

Green Teams Defined:

What is a Green Team?   Any group of people that have come together to work on some project or initiative that achieves some part of their Sustainably Green Principles. There is no ideal set-up. It is a function of the way groups come together, the activities they can do, and the impact they hope to achieve. A Green Team can be formed for one project for a single day, a group that meets regularly to work through a progressive plan…and everything in between. Anyone can participate as long as it doesn't compromise their safety or violate laws. You know – no 10 year olds using the power saw, or unlicensed people re-wiring a light fixture.

To get things started, you need to form a group that will support your needs. I recommend you start one at your head office that encourages staff at all levels to meet on a lunch break once or twice a month to start working on a plan. This group consists of staff, volunteers and members/clients who are passionate about going green. For our "head office" team, only staff participated. Other sites had a combination of volunteers, members and staff. For big events, we recruited from our communities to help. There are many ways to organize.

As you grow additional teams at other locations you will extend your shared learning and start to build a network of Green Teams within your organization. The philosophy behind building Green Teams is that a commitment to sustainability must come from the top but ideas and solutions come from diverse areas throughout your organization.

By having a Green Team at every location, ideas for sustainability can be generated across your organization's areas of influence. Your role and responsibility will be to facilitate communication between the Green Teams to bring a consistent approach and remain in alignment with the Executive team.

As your network grows, the leaders from each team will form a central green "braintrust" that will act as your internal advisors for the organization. Leader representation should be obtained from all levels, and I encourage middle management or up-and-comers to be nominated as leaders. Green Team leaders act as a conduit to communicate the main principles of the green initiatives and strategy to their team members at the various locations and to give voice to everyone's ideas. It is a great way to give opportunity to the future leaders of your organization.

One of the sources of feedback I usually get at this point is: oohhh, another committee with more meetings...uugggh! You don't have to reinvent a structure that already exists if you're your organization supports it, piggyback a Green Team meeting on the last 15 to 20 minutes of your monthly staff meeting for discussion and idea gathering, and let those who want to dig into the projects stay on. Use your existing infrastructure to accelerate the development of this network. Remember, the dividends will pay off to the entire organization, we have made it to the other side and it is better than I could have imagined!

Philosophy of Green Teams - the secret Master Plan

The Green Team structure is based on that of a democratic government (I will borrow the American model), right back to the Declaration of Independence. Each person has the "unalienable rights" to "life, liberty and pursuit of happiness". Cheesy, but the model has some benefits that work in our favor.

The ultimate goal that we strive towards is to have every person understand the repercussions of their decisions and to have created a collective behavioral change to living more sustainably. As with a democracy, there is a list of principles (constitution) that dictate the environment that we live in.

These collectively developed and centrally supported principles rely on the "people" to implement them as well as to challenge them. As we set up Green Teams, we are creating representation in a micro-democracy where each site or location can be likened to a State or Province. The Green Team leaders are the "elected officials" (although we often designate, not elect the initial leaders) who will understand the principles (in this case, the Sustainably Green principles) and work to bring other like-minded people together to affect change as well as report the conditions, hopes, dreams, and successes of their "constituents" to the Executive team through you.

As the groups get bigger, you will be connecting the local corporate CSR teams to the site Green Teams to create a community green team that becomes the foundation of your organization's strategic partnership with the corporate community and individual philanthropists.

As more Green Teams form with the support of the existing teams and start-up tool kits, the leaders will share their ideas and begin to work together on larger regional activities, thus creating a culture of being green in a way that promotes ongoing education, inclusiveness, and advances the core mission of your charity in coordination with your strategic partners.

In short, creating Green Teams will:

- Empower the people who have access to the way your organization and ultimately the surrounding community works;

- Arm them with the philosophy of becoming Sustainably Green;

- Provide them with the tools to understand how to identify and reduce the waste;

- Give them voice to speak about new ideas and a channel for communication.

Green Teams will:

- Provide the resource s to activate the "many hands make quick work" philosophy;

- Acquire the education to "pay it forward" elsewhere in their lives;

- Provide the healthy tension to challenge the organization if it strays from the vision or moves too slowly;

- Becomes the critical link to lasting change to your community.

Structure of a Green Team:

There are basically two styles you should consider for the team structure: Committee and Activity.

Committee-Style Team:

A committee-style team is a group that comes together on a periodic basis to identify, organize and achieve your goals. I recommend that each team have co-chairs – one staff person and one member or community volunteer. It helps to marry the internal mission and workings with the external perspective; as well, it shares the time commitment. As teams get bigger, you can nominate other positions as appropriate. Teams should plan to meet once or twice a month, with sub-groups meeting at cycles that are appropriate for specific projects.

For any meetings, there should be a time, a place, a clear agenda and a clear mandate. Your mandate can be simple, but focused. You want your meetings to be about getting things done, not sessions for people to complain and then leave unfocused and without clear goals. A mandate can be as simple as:

To reduce our "Environmental Footprint" in a way that promotes community engagement to learn from, educate and improve the health of our communities following the principles outlined in the Sustainably Green Principles. We will prioritize our efforts as first improving how we use our spaces, then our buildings, then our neighborhoods, and finally our communities. We will provide leadership and act as a positive role model in sustainability practices.

As with any meeting, value people's time and stick to the agenda. For a committee-style team, the agenda should be simple:

- Welcome & Introductions

- Update on Action Items from last meeting,

- Main Agenda Item or Speaker

- Review of Action Items and plan for next meeting

It is good to have some time for brainstorming ideas, but leave that at the end to ensure the action-based agenda is completed first. You should record a basic set of minutes that lists who attended, lists the length of the meeting (to capture volunteer time), documents the previous successes and Action Items for the next agenda.

This can be written on a standard form or just in an email. I recommend these "minutes" are sent to a central email to allow volunteers to collect, assimilate and redistribute the ideas. In my experience, these volunteers love to see what is being done, and then share the major trends with all groups in periodic updates. You can also just post on a shared network drive, intranet or website (e.g. Google Docs) to let other Green Teams peruse for ideas. Create a Green Team Facebook page to get more people in the discussion.

Activity-Style Team:

An activity-style team is a group that forms for short-term goal to plan and organize specific events or activities. These groups attract people who are interested in accomplishing a specific goal over a short time period as their schedule or interests allow. We find this format brings many more people out and fits better into most peoples' busy lives.

As with any activity, you need to have a leader, either volunteer or staff, who is responsible for achieving the goal of the event. You need to coordinate with your volunteer teams to become intimately familiar with your rules and processes for working with and hosting volunteers.

Similar to the committee-style Green Teams, I recommend that you capture the names and hours worked of volunteers on a sign-in sheet for the event. This is a simple way to record volunteer hours and to show impact. As your projects get a bit more robust, you will need to incorporate liability waivers. Work with your insurer to confirm you are not creating a new liability for your organization.

Green Team Meeting Topics and Activities:

The people on the team, through their experiences and motivations, will drive the work plan of the team. You will find unlimited resources on the Internet, in books, and in the minds of your staff and community members for develop your agenda topics.

When prioritizing topics, I am a big fan of cleaning up your own backyard before you start to peer into other yards. Building experience updating your building or space will give you the confidence to speak with conviction from your own direct experience and the credibility you need to build the momentum within and then outside your walls.

The priorities of the team are to focus first on developing a team of critical mass, and then to start learning and greening the physical spaces in the building. Working through a progression of activities that are also transferrable to homes and businesses elsewhere is a great way to begin as the team can start impacting their spaces immediately, see some early successes and develop cohesiveness as a team.

As you get into the facility systems, the changes won't be immediate as it takes time to build resources (and sometimes expertise). But, the sequence of learning about the green project, assessing what is there, creating some simple "business cases" (justifications for change) and creating the list of what remains to be done is low cost, but high-impact. Think of it as the "honey-do" list to be handed to your maintenance person. As more and more items are discovered, the Green Teams create more and more pressure to drive change.

Once the in-building audits and projects are exhausted, the Green Teams can look to the exterior of the building at sites and in recreation spaces, and then into local recreation and community spaces. Start looking to work with local businesses to share the learnings (maybe justify their savings as a donation to your charity?), arrange "Recycling Days" to encourage people to bring their batteries, electronics, etc. for proper disposal, find a park or school that needs some rejuvenation, clean-up or even restoration.

As the Green Team starts to fully mature, it can work towards regional events such as the "Great Shoreline Cleanup", Earth Day events, World Wildlife Fund's (WWF's) Earth Hour. As they reach into local businesses, government and other institutions, they can link together on these larger community and regional events.

Green Team Agenda Items:

A typical order of progression might look like:

▪ Shade-O-Green Assessment and related outcomes will be used to build a list of agenda items.

▪ Meetings with Food – create a protocol for reduced single-use containers, cutlery and plates/bowls. Maybe even move to a standard of locally grown and prepared food.

▪ Recycling Audit

  o Perform a deeper assessment.

  o Implement programs throughout the organization to include plastics, glass, paper, organics and batteries to start.

  o Future stages can (and should) include: electronics (monitors, CPUs, peripherals, laptops, etc) and light bulbs (fluorescent, CFLs).

▪ Printer Paper at the Office

  o Review and improve the type currently used: % recycled, Eco-Logo & FSC certification, locality of source.

  o Improve the efficiency of use: double-sided printing, wasteful printing projects, amount of marketing and print materials created and circulated.

  o Invoices and payments: checks, electronic payments for business transactions and staff payments.

▪ Water Consumption

  o Perform a deeper assessment at all locations.

  o Create a standard for faucets, showers, toilets, urinals with facilities teams.

  o

- Electrical Consumption from Lighting

  o Perform a deeper assessment at all locations. Break it up to divide and conquer: CFL audit, old fluorescent lighting audit, switch audit, etc.

  o Replace easy bulbs with CFLs or LEDs while maintaining equivalent wattage.

  o Create a standard for new fixtures with facilities teams.

  o Identify rooms that could use a Smart Switch – auto sensors that will turn on and off the lights.

  o Implement a "Turn off the Lights" program.

- Electrical Consumption from Plug-In Appliances

  o Perform a deeper assessment at all locations.

  o Add power bars to allow easy turnoff.

  o Implement a "Turn off Your Tools" program.

  o Identify energy hogs (e.g. refrigerators, computers, monitors, etc.)

- Energy Consumption from Heating and Cooling

  o Perform a deeper assessment at all locations (include facility staff.)

  o Find old thermostats.

  o Create a standard for new programmable thermostats with facilities teams.

  o Double check that the programming is actually working.

  o Look for wasted heat in the summer (are the heaters by the windows on at the same time as the air conditioner? …In my experience, 10 to 25% of the time, this is happening in older buildings.)

- ▪ Cleaning Chemicals
  - ○ Perform a deeper assessment at all locations.
  - ○ Look for Eco-Logo or Green Seal logos.
  - ○ Create a standard for new greener cleaning chemicals with facilities teams.

<u>Green Culture Projects</u>

a. Speakers – look for opportunities to bring in a speaker to focus on a topic about your charitable mission with a slant towards the environmental impacts.

b. Bring in "How-To" speakers that can educate people in your organization and invite the community too.

c. Invite your suppliers and vendors to come in and "sell" their Environmental or Sustainability products or programs that are already in-use or can be moved towards (e.g. paper products, marketing materials, lights, water appliances, etc.)

d. Set up a community walk to assess your communities green spaces and poorly used areas to plan future restoration or clean-up events.

e. Set up a community walk to assess your communities commercial and retail businesses to see how they are doing on being Sustainably Green. Maybe work out some donations for some volunteer work to assess to fix the easy items.

This is merely a starter list. There are endless resources out there, and the really cool ideas will come from your teams as they recognize things that can be changed. Tweet other ideas to @givinggreen "green team topic"

 Example: hey @givinggreen other "**green team topic**" should be commuting and bike to work.

One of my favorite projects was developing green team event t-shirts. The YMCA of Greater Toronto has a small high school, the YMCA Academy that is an alternative school to help kids with learning challenges who have fallen through the cracks of the traditional schools and need more holistic approach to learning. These are amazing kids that have often struggled in their home lives and previous schools, but possess incredible skills and minds.

One of the staff members, Craig, worked with the students to repurpose left-over event t-shirts and as "Green Team" shirts - they were printed but not used. Craig worked with some amazing silk-screening artwork, but didn't turn them inside out – they were highlighting the fact that these were unused printed shirts and to be reused to brand the Green Teams. The Academy's art program had become a production house for our Green Team shirts. Truly inspirational!

Jump Start Approach:

The approach that I just described is the recipe for success for most organizations as it builds a foundation and capacity. It takes existing staff teams and people familiar with organizing committees or events, and builds up awareness and impact in an incremental manner. On some sites, it just doesn't work based on the nature of the programs, staff or that one amazing leader doesn't emerge.

An alternate "jump-start" approach is to rally your staff, members, clients and volunteers around a specific inspirational project. You are creating rapid awareness and focus around an eye-catching event or activity that can enlist the people into your Green Teams.

When we started the Green Roof at the Central YMCA in downtown Toronto, we didn't have a Green Team at that location. I worked with the site staff to form an impromptu team that was excited about our green roof vision and could mobilize their community around that idea. As you re-read the brief description of this project in **Chapter 1: The Concept and Why This Works**, with this in-mind, you can see how momentum was built, a team formed, and some incredible volunteers that had developed a vested interest in the project wanted to remain connected to steward that space along.

It also drew in all of the other elements that I have been discussing: large scale volunteerism, major corporate donations, a community that learned about both ecology and environmental technology and how it can co-exist in an urban environment. We still use many of the ideas discussed in the first half of this chapter, just not in the same sequence. There is no wrong way to do it.

Embedding your Learning into Your Programs:

As your find different solutions, look for different ways to blend them back into your programming so that you embed sustainability into your charitable programs. This has endless opportunities and there are numerous resources online to get the ball rolling. A few examples that we have done at the YMCA of Greater Toronto are:

1. **Green Pre-School Education Segment:** Developed a "Green" supplement to our "Playing to Learn" curriculum that has become a national standard for childcare education in Canada. We hired an intern into a position that was federally funded and they worked through our existing curriculum and blended in important lessons on energy, water, earth, planting and other themes, including play-based activities to get the little ones physically engaged.

2. **Green Teenager Activity Guide:** YMCA Canada developed a list of activities targeted at teenagers to educate them through group activities that are used in youth leadership sessions, camping and in our YMCA Academy (high school). The program was designed to be youth-led and adult supported.

3. **Self-Employment Class:** We developed a class on the importance of incorporating sustainability when starting up a business. This new class was added to the larger self-employment program that we run to help individuals learn about starting up a business. This new class takes the time to consider how these new business owners will impact on the planet, use energy, commute, access resources, and structuring their employer benefits for hiring and retaining staff.

4. **Outdoor Day and Overnight Camp:** Integrating environmental leadership into an existing outdoor education camp located in a unique ecological area helped to expand our camping education to include a broader approach to environmental learning. It has an organic farm and is integrating modern environmental technology into an ecologically protected space, coexisting to the benefit of the community of regional biodiversity.

Action Items:

1.   Build a Green Team. Start at your place of business to be able to see how to form it. Depending on your current role, you might want to lead this first team, or find a person in your organization or a volunteer to take ownership of this task.

2.   Use social media to attract new members. It's a great way to find younger volunteers who have more time on their hands. Maybe access volunteers from local high schools who need to gain volunteer hours.

3.   Connect with the leaders at different program sites and try to find a way to build a new Green Team or leverage an existing structure to get ideas flowing. Have one person designated as the hub of environmental activities and projects.

4.   Find a volunteer to organize the minutes and start to pull together different tasks and activities that can be shared among the Green Teams.

5.   Tweet your thoughts:

@givinggreen – we held our first "green team" meeting

@giving green – another great "green team" topic is to bring a water bottle to work event

Knowledge is no guarantee of good behavior, but ignorance is a virtual guarantee of bad behavior
    - Martha Nussbaum

How many legs does a dog have if you call the tail a leg? Four. Calling a tail a leg doesn't make it a leg.
    - Abraham Lincoln

Chapter 13 – Improving Your Building Systems

If you think back to the **Chapter 10: Building Your Green Fund**, you will remember that I asked you to think through the example of replacing traditional incandescent lights with compact fluorescent lights (CFLs) as a way to open your eyes to reducing your consumption, saving energy and ultimately reducing your carbon footprint.

We will now focus on the entire building and enlist your key people: your maintenance team, your facilities team, your service contractors – your technical experts! This is the team you call when the building is too cold, the lights give off that annoying flicker, your faucet stops giving water – these are the magicians who make your building come alive.

Assembling Your Project List:

Each building or space is different and the knowledge of the maintenance teams will vary. While in **Chapter 2: Defining Your Shade of Green**, you were trying to get a sense of where your organization was on the green spectrum, now you are working with the maintenance team to build a comprehensive list of projects and assemble the projects in your Green Fund.

How you gather this information will also vary by your size, budget and expertise.

Stage 1: Doing it on the Cheap

This is where most organizations should start. It relies on your existing team of staff and service contractors to put together a list of projects following certain themes. This will also give your facility staff a chance to demonstrate what they have done and to describe some of their plans. Make sure you take this chance to thank them for their behind-the-scenes work, for accomplishing what they have done so far with limited (or no) support, and then seek their help building this plan. At the YMCA, this is where I started, working closely with the facility staff, and working with them to build lists. We worked closely to develop business cases to justify spending more money on these facilities to help them operate better, save money, and reduce our impact.

The external contractors that look after your building are also a valuable resource for identifying projects and solutions. While they should be incented to raise issues to get more work, I can't tell you the number of times that a contractor said, "I didn't think you guys had any money or cared, so we stopped telling you about this kind of thing." Use their knowledge of your building to build your plan and even to help set budgets. If you are concerned that their solutions may not be the best approach, then ask a competing contractor to offer an alternative solution.

Stage 2: Finding Low-Cost Help

After some initial investigation, I prefer to turn this type of activity into a "Living Laboratory" to engage external volunteers or low-cost help to perform some thorough inspections.

For the YMCA, we built a partnership with a local technical college (Sheridan College) that provided a flock of students to perform energy assessments of our major buildings. Their work included their time in the field with knowledgeable professors, as well as time to investigate and get grants to pay for their time as well as future work. They have gained real world experience as part of their course work and the professors didn't have to develop mock examples – these were field trips on real-world problems!

An alternate approach would be to find individual volunteers to do this similar work under the leadership of the maintenance team. This second stage actually builds on the work of the first stage.

Stage 3: Hire a consultant

This is the fastest way to get this information into your hands. It costs more, but you are dealing with professionals and getting information that is current and thorough. Some organizations start at this stage, others work their way through the different stages and then strategically add consultants. We have had some success getting consultants to offer some of their services pro-bono or deeply discounted as part of this strategy.

Green Culture on Existing Buildings

How do you get these teams to understand, to believe in this change, and to remain committed? When I meet with other facility teams as part of the YMCA family, we talk about the activities that pertain to how we operate and renew our facilities from the perspective of asset and procurement teams. Changes to the buildings are one of the highest impact for the lowest cost to reducing your organization's environmental footprint. It is the proverbial low-hanging fruit.

It is important to demonstrate to these teams that there is a larger strategy to drive a cultural change to becoming green, that this will be something that is planned to take multiple years, and your organization will remain committed. The model I prefer for driving any kind of change across a large group: Top-Down, Bottom-Up, Middle-Out.

The "Top-Down" strategy is where most cultural change starts; with the leadership or Executive team setting the overall vision and principles. Sadly, for many organizations, this is done in a vacuum and then is shared with the staff. When done properly, there is an engagement process that includes key user groups to properly define this vision.

When the "Bottom-Up" part of this model is engaged, the front-line staff and volunteers (who have access to the problems and solutions) are allowed to help innovate and bring forth ideas. Their knowledge becomes critical in crafting the right solutions. This group is part of the implementation of the solutions – they are the real drivers of the cultural and behavioral change. When done right, you give this group a voice in the change.

The "Middle-Out" is where the facilities teams sit alongside other managers. When it comes to the buildings, the maintenance and facility teams have to carefully "manage up" to create consensus, and "manage down" to standardize and drive implementation, and finally, "manage externally" to ensure the contractors meet the standards. Overall, this "middle-out" approach is the glue that holds the process together.

Top Down Steps:

To highlight the discussion thus far, we have completed the following:

- o We created the Sustainably Green Principles – a set of principles that highlights how we can make changes that will have a positive impact on the environment. It defines our green lens.
- o We created and updated our Annual Implementation Plan to define our short term goals.
- o We created a Sustainability Advisory Counsel, made up of industry leaders.
- o We have measured our Environmental Footprint
- o Established Sustainability Goals for our Association
- o We have developed a Green Fund to seek donations to fund these activities. Next step, we need to build a suite of projects to put into the Green-Giving Fund and achieve to our goals.

Bottom Up Steps:

At the field level, we established a series of Green Teams that are working on a shared mandate that extends across all sites, has some central support from the Environmental Coordinator creating and shared tools and resources. The typical progression is to first improve the operations in all staff areas, then into member and participant areas and across the entire building in coordination with the facility staff.

The next layer is to look externally to the buildings in the direct neighborhood, and to eventually extend further out to connect with other Green Teams, both internally and externally to undertake more community projects.

Volunteerism is the vehicle that drives all of this work, and we seek this not only from staff and members who want to play a part in achieving our goals, but also with external philanthropic partners, ideally with a financial gift. We have seen this as an important element of a strategic partnership that yields repeat donations and volunteer engagements.

In a few years, if all goes according to plan, the Green Teams will actually have the greatest impact in finding ways to ensure we become Sustainably Green. They are the source of innovation.

Bottom Up Steps:

1.　　Engaged Facility Teams

2.　　Established Green Teams

　　　　A.　　Nominate a Chair (staff & volunteer co-chairs)

　　　　B.　　Provide Start-up Tools

　　　　C.　　Link in to other Green Teams

　　　　D.　　Work internally, then externally

　　　　E.　　Major Resource in the Green Projects

Working from the Middle-Out:

While Senior Management drives strategy from the top down, front line staff feed ideas up, develop projects and then seek support from the "Middle" group (facilities teams, procurement teams, other key managers). These "Middle" teams provide the technical knowledge and project management skills to help develop the best solution. They also have the team that drives standards and moves toward consistency of service and products to derive all the benefits that can be achieved through buying power, consistency of training, less inventory, and so on. Clearly, this team can be multiple groups for larger organizations or a "team of one" for smaller ones. It is about responsibility, not size.

Minor Changes to Your Building (operational projects)

There are many small things that can be done that will create significant cost and energy savings. We looked at a small example in **Chapter 10: Creating your Green Fund**. This following list contains a bunch of projects we did with some budget costing of prices. This is not exhaustive, but a good starting point.

Lighting Improvements:

1.   Replace incandescent with CFLs (or LEDs, if costs make sense)

- Everywhere, do it all at once.

2.   Update exit signs to LED

- Convert existing - LED Lamp ($45; 2-year payback)

- Replace exit sign – plastic ($50 + install)

- Replace exit sign – aluminum ($150 + install)

3.   Replace switches with motion sensors

- Small mechanical rooms and storage rooms

- Janitor's closets and pipe chases

- Any other space that is used intermittently, which can include restrooms, meeting rooms, etc.

Gas Improvements:

1.   Review mechanical equipment (with HVAC service technician)

- Identify and resolve "by-passed" settings. These are systems that have some kind of brain to help control the use of the mechanical device. When it is set in "by-pass" mode, it means that something is not working properly and this manual setting is by-passing the controls. This should be fixed or resolved since the unit is continuously on in this mode rather than not turning off based on some defined logic.

- Add building control logic or Building Automation Systems (BAS) to properly control the use of newer mechanical systems. Assuming that there is already an existing BAS in the building, it is very common for buildings that replace a specific mechanical unit (boiler, air handling unit, etc.) to have had them installed without connecting it into the existing BAS. This means that as the building is controlled for different conditions, this new mechanical unit is not part of the conversation.

You might hear "Oh, that unit has its own control system" or a "standalone" control. This means that there is some logic built in that controls when the mechanical unit comes on, but it still remains disconnected from the main system. Whenever a change occurs, someone has to manually walk over to that unit and also change the settings (if they remember or have time). I recommend that you get a cost or quote to have the mechanical unit connected to your main BAS and then you can make the decision about the cost-benefit.

If you don't have a BAS, this should be added to your Project List.

- Clean and repair dampers, ducts and coils. This is like cleaning the air filter in the car, the filter on your furnace, the lint from the back of your hairdryer or the hair from your brush. This needs to be done, or it stops working well and you are throwing away a lot of gas or electricity and creating safety concerns. We have found examples of gas savings of 25 to 40 percent based on dirty heating and cooling coils.

If you don't know what a damper is, have your maintenance person show one to you. You can think of it like the airflow control on the dashboard of your car that changes the amount of air that blows in your face. These are either manual or automatic. In old buildings, the automatic ones get broken and then the airflow starts to get wasted in some areas. Fix them!

- Turn off heaters and other devices off-season. Seriously, I walk around buildings in the summer and check those little electrical heaters by the window and feel the heat. I realize I am kind of weird to be touching radiators in other people's building, but I hate seeing this!

<u>Improving Paper Impacts:</u>

1.   Move to double-sided printing

2.   Printer paper and office supplies

- FSC Certified for new wood products

- Eco-Label certified for any products

3.   Paper towels and toilet paper

- Look at the larger format dispensers and percentage of recycling materials

- Use products that have FSC and Eco Logo certifications

<u>Water Improvements:</u>

1.   Reduce swimming pool dumps (from 2 to 4 years)…assuming you have a pool, we have lots at the Y!

- Include an assessment of the materials and procedures used for grouting and re-grouting your tiles

- Be more diligent on how the pool chemistry is managed, this affects the rate of degradation of all you pool systems, including tiles, grout, pipes, and the people that use these spaces.

2.   Replace water appliances and devices

- Update faucet aerators to 0.5 GPM (cascade)

- Update showers to 2.5 GPM (or try 2 GPM)

- Replace toilets to 6 LPF

- Replace urinals to 3.8 LPF

3.   Improve Cleaning Chemicals

- Move to a Green Seal solution to both improve your cleaning effectiveness, reduce your costs, and increases the safeness for the people cleaning as well as the people around it. This will also create less of a problem when it is washed down the drain to your local watershed.

- Look at your cleaning tools (e.g. micro fibre) and powered machines.

4. Laundry soap dispensers and solutions

- Consider moving to a system that uses less water and is automated with a soap dispenser system. We found that we saved money, time, were able to track our laundry and had a net improvement on the environment. We moved to a solution that has reduced our water consumption, uses smaller containers that are recyclable, is more effective, has lower water temperature/gas costs, and is better for the environment.

Recycling Improvements:

While you need to have the right receptacles in the right places with good signs to explain what goes in them; if there is nothing behind the scenes that takes that hard work and properly disposes of those items in the right way, it is all for nothing – just another form of greenwashing.

- Standardize paper, plastic and glass collection

- Add an organics recycling program

- Recycle batteries

- Properly dispose of major equipment and program equipment (electronics and metal scrap)

- Properly dispose of fluorescent tubes and CFLs (lighting suppliers)

- Hazardous chemicals should be properly identified and removed

Forest and Green Space Management Improvements:

1. Landscaping maintenance projects. Organize your annual work in a way that will allow for volunteers to help.

2. As you renovate or make changes, replant at least three trees for each removed tree. And tree type matters, understand your local ecology and what is needed.

3. Enhance paved areas - look for poorly used spaces that can be "greened" up.

4. Create gardens and community green spaces.

Major Changes to Your Building (Capital Projects)

As we move into capital projects, the list can be long, and will rely on how well you understand your building. While you might still be reeling from the list of "minor changes" detailed in the last section, working through those changes will get the right people looking at the right systems. They will find other items that were not listed. They will find that some of these systems can't be fixed and need to be replaced.

This is good - this is where you want to start. It makes a lot of sense to start replacing your broken systems with current efficient ones before you start replacing systems that are operating. This is a healthy renewal done in an energy-efficient way, and it allows you to be planful in seeking maximum grants and payback.

Following the same theme as above, here are some sample projects from the YMCA of Greater Toronto:

Electrical Improvements:

1. Convert Fluorescent Lights - T12 to T8

We reused the lighting fixture and just replaced the smart parts fixtures (the bulb types and ballasts) to convert the light to a more efficient system. We converted 287 - T12 fixtures to T8 lights. For our example:

- Installation Cost: $41,000 for fixtures and installation
- The conversion saved 43% consumption (~$6,600/yr)

- Incentive of $400/kW saved ($5,800) from power authority (LDC)
- Partially funded (67% capital cost) by stimulus grant
- Payback was 5 years (excluding stimulus)

2.   Convert Fluorescent Lights – HID to LED

One of the Ys replaced their metal halide pool lights with LED lights. They replaced 24 - 1000 Watt (indirect), 8 - 400 Watt (direct) metal halide fixtures with 16 - 146 Watt (direct) LED Fixtures. For our example:

- Installation Cost: $27,500 fixtures, $2,500 labor for installation
- The conversion saved 92% consumption (~$16,000/yr)
- Payback was less than 2 years

3.   Install a Lighting Control System
Install a computer system that controls when your lights go on and off.

4.   High Power Equipment Changes

Power Factor Correction: After you have done the major electrical changes to your building, you may find that there are significant savings available based on how efficiently your building distributes electricity throughout your building. You are actually penalized by your power company based on your "power factor" or efficiency of using the electricity within the distribution network. Without getting too technical, there are changes that can be made to your high-power systems that enables less of the electricity to be wasted in the wires and controllers.

Gas Improvements:

As you look at your energy spending, you will find that gas is a major contributor; especially the further north you live. These mechanical systems have made huge technology improvements in the last 10 years and now use considerably less gas. They are also very expensive systems to replace. Building a list of the mechanical gas-guzzlers that are at the end of their life and due for replacement is the best place to start. When you are making decisions about what type of "high-efficiency" system to use, I recommend you use the Life-Cycle approach to costing. Don't just consider the short-term one-time cost.

1.   **Retro-commissioning:** As you spend time with your service contractors, a discussion of "retro-commissioning" is bound to come up. What this means is that an experienced HVAC technician can spend a certain amount of time reviewing your mechanical systems and put everything back to the proper settings. This is a very good thing to do, like getting a tune-up on your car. At the Y, we have found exceptional savings in our older buildings, from 10 to 40 percent savings; plus, we have found lots of grants and incentives to reduce this cost.

2.   **Replace Boilers:** These systems heat the water for your buildings. The hot water is either used in your taps and showers, or is used for heating spaces through radiators. Modern boilers consume significantly less gas and often have huge incentives or grants available to offset the replacement costs.

3.   **Replace Chillers:** These help to keep your building cool in the summer. Modern technology is much more efficient and is built to come on in stages, depending on your cooling needs.

4.   **Update Cooling Towers with a Variable Speed Drive (VSD):** This works together with the chillers to keep you building cool in the summer using just the right amount of energy.

5.   **Install a Building Automation System (BAS**): This is a brain that controls the equipment and spaces throughout the building. It is difficult to calculate the payback since the waste is widely distributed throughout the building, but it is a very good project to pursue. At the Y, we have received grants based on 10 to 20 percent reductions of gas consumption with success.

6.   **Replace Pre-heating Coils with Heat Recovery Units:** Heating coils are typically electrical heaters that have been installed in your ductwork. At the Y, we have worked with engineers to design systems that replace the heating coils with a technology that takes the heat out of the air that is being exhausted outside. You recover the heat from the air that was previously heated and use that energy to heat the outside air in the winter to warm it up on the way inside.

7.   **Install Solar Thermal Arrays:** As we dug through our mechanical rooms, we found that there were some systems that were no longer needed and could be re-purposed for more modern technology. For

example, at the Y, we had a new boiler that didn't require us to store as much hot water because the boiler was able to keep up with the demand and wasting energy to store the hot water. We took two large storage tanks from that system and reused them as part of a glazed solar-thermal array – which means we heat the water using the sun, through the solar panels, and then store that hot water in these un-used storage tanks. Thanks to a large grant and some creative thinking, we were able to reuse an old system as part of an alternate technology.

At a different site, we were able to secure funding to install an unglazed solar-thermal array (black pipe on the roof) that heats our pool water and laundry boilers in the summer months.

8. **Install Waste Heat Recovery on our Pools:** We were able to install a system that takes the heat out of the waste pool water and use it to reheat the new water coming into the pool. This was partially funded through a grant which gave us a one-year payback and significant annual savings.

Green Procurement:

I would be remiss if I didn't mention one of the key underpinning strategies you should ensure is embedded into your organization – understanding the environmental impact of what you buy. The first reaction most people give when I mention Green Procurement is – is costs more! This isn't always the case, it's about being aware of what you are buying and incorporating that information into your buying decision. Procurement in general is about establishing what you find valuable, and then asking vendors to inform you about how their product or service impacts you buying goals. Too often, the decision starts and stops with the cost, but it extends to many other areas like: reliability, ease of use, quality, support and training, etc.

If you are interested in delving into the world of procurement strategies, there are many fantastic books and resources out there – my comments here are that you need to consider the environmental impacts, finding your green lens. This will be built into your standards and allow you to consider the environmental impacts along with the many other buying goals you will have.

Action Items:

1.   This chapter is all about working with the facility staff in your organization. Almost all of the people in this field will be so excited to have this conversation with you as the information presented in this chapter is what they are fighting against day in and day out. Working though this chapter with that key individual will require time and likely some great technical volunteers or extra hours from the staff. As this list gets built and added to the Green Fund list of projects, it will grow rapidly.

2.   Consider reaching out to a local consultant to see if they can support work in this chapter as your facility staff hits some barriers.

3.   Tweet your thoughts:

 @givinggreen other "building systems" you should include are…

We live in a society exquisitely dependent on science and technology, in which hardly anyone knows anything about science and technology.
- Carl Sagan

What the computer is to me is the most remarkable tool that we have ever come up with. It's the equivalent of a bicycle for our mind.
- Steve Jobs

Chapter 14 – Improving Your Information Technology Systems

Each year, I seem to become more and more reliant on technology. I have always been pretty good with computers and programming, but when I need help, I turn to my family for advice. Back in the late 70s and 80s, most people were starting to enjoy color TVs, while my home was filled with computer geeks – my mother was a computer programmer that led teams of software development and implementation; my dad, a nuclear engineer, was always building complex spreadsheets and models that forecasted that decomposition rate of uranium; and my older brother, Rolf, liked to build and program computers in our basement in his free time.

My lessons in the world of computers started as I joined Rolf on his visits to computer fairs and competitions. He would buy chips, boards, and all the bits that make up a computer, and then actually make it work. I learned some programming, but as I went on to learn more about structural and civil engineering, Rolf followed his passion into the Naval Academy as an electrical engineer. He worked as an officer in the Navy on submarines, and later started a now thriving business with his wife in Atlanta helping companies develop their Information Systems (IT). He is the guy your IT people turn to when they want to know about the next step in running their business – the IT guy for the IT guys.

So naturally, as I started to write about all the waste that exists in our buildings, my brother Rolf had tons of advice. In his words, here is what he had to say:

Going Green in Technology

As you are going around your organization changing out light bulbs, adding insulation, removing space heaters from underneath desks, there they sit, blinking their baleful green eyes at you, taunting you with supposed untouchability. Yes, I am talking about the computers on everyone's desk.

Is this realm really untouchable? Are the high priests of Information Technology (IT) going to dismiss your efforts with some technobabble? I think not!

Let's break the IT systems down and figure out what we can do to make them more efficient. Actually, the desktop computers are the just the tip of the iceberg. There are a lot of back-end systems that are hidden out of sight which are ripe for energy savings as well. From a high level, they can be divided into three functional areas:

1.   **Datacenter systems.** These are all the boxes in the air-conditioned, halon protected temple of Information Technology. The datacenter contains servers, storage, network, and data security systems, all oriented toward the goal of running applications that end users can access and can use to do their job.

2.   **Distributed infrastructure**. This is the network, wireless network, security systems, access control, backup power, and air conditioning of all the equipment in place to allow end user systems to connect to the datacenter.

3.   **End user systems.** These are the PC's, laptops, tablets, phones, point of sale terminals, card readers, and LCD screens that individual users interact with on a regular basis

These systems all use electrical power and generate heat, requiring air conditioning, which of course uses more power. Most people would be surprised at the large amounts of energy needed to power our modern information technology. Since there is always progress in Information Systems, let's talk about some newer ways of doing things that can significantly reduce the power used.

At this point you may be thinking this will be an uphill battle and that the denizens of the IT shop would be against your effort. Wrong! In just about every case, they will be your wholehearted supporters. They love playing with new technology, they stay on top of new developments, and if you are a willing partner who will work to help them fund and socialize system upgrades, expect them to jump for joy!

The next thing you are thinking is that this will be very complex. Well, just like you would not plan on designing and constructing an entire new building by yourself, don't plan on going through this process alone either.

There is an equivalent to construction companies in the Information Technology world. They are called IT Solutions Providers, and for any of these initiatives you identify, they can assess your current situation, provide budgetary pricing for an upgrade, show how the new systems can save money and improve operations, and conduct the entire upgrade from start to finish.

If you have not worked with IT Solutions Providers before, no problem, I have included a section on how to get what you want from an IT upgrade project. It describes the principles that apply not only to IT, but to most new project sourcing you may want to conduct.

Datacenter Systems:

Once you have finished a cup of coffee with your IT person, the best place to start your journey is with a tour of the Datacenter systems. The main purpose of these systems is to reliably provide applications to users – email, finance systems, shared files. In order to work, the Datacenter systems have a combination of hardware and software working together in a redundant and reliable fashion. Over the years, systems have gotten progressively more power efficient, and there are new ways of delivering these applications. As with building systems, the change had been so dramatic, that rethinking how it works will save money, time and energy costs.

Just remember as you go through these exercises and analyses, that there are certain goals the IT staff have. Among them are:

1.   Keep the systems up and running.
2.   Don't lose any data.

3.   Don't violate any private information security guidelines.
4.   Keep users happy.
5.   Upgrade systems to make things work better and more cost effectively.

If they are not able to accomplish items 1-3, then there will be an issue, sometimes even a "resume-generating" event, as we call it. As long as you keep in mind the above priorities, the IT staff will be your whole-hearted supporters.

Within the Datacenter, there are different decisions that can be made that start to consolidate the amount of equipment you have or even start to move these system out of the Datacenter. Three strategies that have emerged over the last five to fifteen years are:

1.   Server Virtualization
2.   Application Conversion
3.   Applications in the Cloud

Server Virtualization

It used to be that one physical server would be used for each application. Since a typical organization runs between 10 and 100 applications, and many of them need to be clustered for reliability (duplicated for redundancy), that means anywhere from 20 to 200 servers. Examples of applications are an email server, an accounting server, a Point of Sale server, or other things like that.

In the mid 2000's, server virtualization combined with more powerful servers to reduce a 200 server datacenter to about 16 physical servers. With each server power supply averaging 300 Watts, and two per server, that's a power reduction from 120,000 Watts down to 9,600 Watts! Since these servers are running 24/7, that becomes a savings of over $100,000 per year in just electrical savings! That does not include the reduction of space, the reduction of Air-Conditioning, 184 fewer servers, and the time saved from running them all.

Server virtualization can be little tricky to understand, and many organizations that have not gone through this are afraid of the change. In simplistic terms, think of it as replacing 200 cars with 16 buses, but everyone gets where they are going just as if they had their own car. Since the cars are all going to the same place, carpooling in the bus gives you one vehicle, albeit a bigger one, with one engine to maintain. As you might expect, it costs money to buy these more powerful servers and the virtualization software needed. It's not just the servers that get upgraded; it's also the server network and the shared storage systems. So there is a significant capital expense.

Some organizations find it easier just to keep paying the monthly electric bill that is in someone else's budget than to spend money on new equipment. So there may be some resistance to making these changes, because many finance people see IT as a cost center, and want to keep the costs as low as possible. This is no longer cutting edge, this is today's approach and the discussion needs to start because server virtualization is the most cost-effective way to cut electricity and cooling costs in the datacenter.

As with the other projects that were looked at within the building, a business case is needed to prove the savings and make this move forward. This is where using your IT Solution Providers can help. They see what a lot of other organizations are doing, and so are sometimes looked upon as more knowledgeable than the internal IT staff of the organization. Let the Solution Providers help you in making the case.

Applications Conversion

The next way to save energy and costs is to move applications from less efficient systems to more efficient ones. For this, you have to expand your idea of what an application is. Any information system in your organization can be converted into an application running on virtualized servers. Look around for special purpose systems, and find out if there are network based equivalents.

Instead of running multiple sets of wires through the walls of your buildings, all applications these days can be run over your data network, also known as your Local Area Network and Wide Area Network.

The phone system is the biggest one. In the early 2000's, organizations started switching from dedicated Private Branch Exchange (PBX) hardware and telephone handsets to network based phone systems. Instead of putting a PBX in every building, you can run your telephone applications on the servers in your datacenter, plug new handsets into your LAN, and have everything running on one reliable network.

This is not a low quality Internet Voice over IP phone system! It is a highly reliable distributed voice system running over your reliable data network. And if your data network is not currently reliable, then part of the network phone system upgrade is to improve your data network until it is reliable.

This type of system can actually pay for itself very quickly. By converting to an IP (Internet Protocol) based phone system, you can change out the connections from the local phone company. Instead of paying every month for a separate data and phone connection, you can just pay for a data connection and have the calls sent over your data network. Doing this uses a technology called SIP trunking. Not every provider in your area may offer it yet, but a few will, so make sure you ask for it.

There are cost savings from lower monthly payments to the phone company, less trips to each location to make changes or repairs to the phone system, and less cabling in a new building. Cost and energy savings depend greatly on your number of locations, cost for phone services, and your existing IT infrastructure.

You can do the same thing with other systems as well:
1. Video conferencing.
2. Video surveillance.
3. Access control.
4. Facilities monitoring and control.
5. Overhead paging.
6. Nurse/Emergency call.

For each of these systems conversions, make sure you seek the support of your internal IT staff, engage vendors who make these types of upgrades all the time, identify the risks, costs, and benefits, then take the appropriate action.

Applications to the Cloud

Not all applications need to run on the servers in your organization's datacenter. Some applications are better off running on somebody else's servers, using their electricity, and having their IT specialists manage and maintain the systems.

The consumption model then changes from purchase and support to a monthly fee. There are many factors that go into making the decision to move to a Cloud application, so each should be done on a case by case basis. For organizations that have not yet made the leap to virtualization, moving to the cloud allows for two hops on the technology spectrum, and the savings exceed those outlined in those business cases.

In the mid-2010's, some examples of common applications that organizations move from on-premise to the cloud are:
1. Email
2. Accounting
3. Customer Relationship Management

Some people believe all applications are going to move to the cloud eventually, and that organizations won't run their own datacenters at all anymore. Others believe organizations will continue to operate internal servers for applications that are core to their business, the loss of which could cause the organization to cease operations. Either way, it is worth looking at for all applications.

Transitioning applications to the cloud should be done with a full analysis of costs, risks, and benefits. There should also be a plan for how to bring the application and data back in house if necessary.

End User Systems

If an organization has 1000 users, and each of them has a PC and screen using an average of 150 Watts of power, that's 150,000 Watts in use. This adds to both the electrical and air conditioning bill, and is a good place to find savings.

There are a few different ways of addressing end-user systems, and it depends on the type of user and the policies of the organization.

Some organizations are moving to a Bring Your Own Device (BYOD) initiative, where workers are able to bring in their own laptops, tablets, and phones, and given access to internal systems using those devices.

Others are moving to Virtual Desktop Infrastructure (VDI), where desktop PC's are replaced by low power thin clients. Moving to thin clients, which have no hard drive and lower power processers, can reduce the 1000 user end device power budget from 150,000 Watts to 50,000. As well, the thin clients have a usable life about twice as long as PC's.

Many organizations are deploying both new models of end user computing. In fact, putting in place VDI enables better BYOD.

There are other benefits to Virtual Desktop Infrastructure as well:
1. Provides a more secure BYOD scenario, because users can only access applications from their own devices using the secured virtual desktop.
2. End user support requires a lot less on-site troubleshooting. If there is a problem with the device, it can just be replaced. Meanwhile, the user can log in from a different device.
3. VDI allows users to work from home just as easily as from the office. This can allow for more flexible working conditions, with possibly lower costs.
4. All of the user's information is backed up on central servers and storage. Less time is spent in recovering lost information.

Just like with server virtualization, converting to virtual desktops requires a capital outlay. There are costs in new servers, storage systems, and applications, as well as the services to convert existing PC's to a virtual PC model. Many organizations find, however, there are significant benefits from a Total Cost of Ownership point of view that they make the conversion to Virtual Desktop Infrastructure.

Just like with any other IT initiative, conduct a pilot project first before committing the organization to a wholesale changeover!

The Information Technology realm is ripe for upgrades that can assist in your Green Initiative. Moving from old to new technology is something your IT staff has probably wanted to do for some time. They should greet your initiatives with a warm welcome, because they should have similar initiatives for server virtualization, application conversion, Bring Your Own Device, and Virtual Desktop Infrastructure.

Action Items:

1.   Find the head of IT for your organization and meet with them to learn about how your organization runs its IT infrastructure. Test some of these ideas to see what has been tried and where they are planning to go. Your goal is to have them outline some new projects (scope and budget) that will appear in the Green Fund as upgrades to bring your IT infrastructure to a more current, leaner and more efficient place.

2.   Try to find a "green" ally on the IT team. Having a key person who understands the goals of becoming Sustainably Green can be a person who opens doors beyond the basic IT infrastructure. They can assist with websites, social media and lots of other IT-related activities.

3.   Check out the bonus chapter at www.givingcharitiesgree.com that you can share with your IT team. This chapter "Secrets for Buying Your Next Big Project from an IT Solution Provider" was also written by Rolf and offers some sage advice for your IT team to consider when starting to upgrade to these newer technologies.

4.   Tweet your thoughts:

 @givinggreen "IT team" let me into the server room – its sooo cold.

The difference between what we do and what we are capable of doing would suffice to solve most of the world's problems.

- Mahatma Gandhi

We can't solve problems by using the same kind of thinking we used when we created them.
- Albert Einstein

Chapter 15 – Inspiring Changes to Your Community

There are few times in my life that I am so awe-inspired, yet feel at complete peace, as when I spend time at the oceanside on a beautiful day. The rolling and repeating percussion of the crashing waves like the bass coupled with timpani in crescendo…and then fading away. It demonstrates such immense power in an elegant and soothing manner - like an African tiger purring and nuzzling against you cheek. You sense the power, but are lulled by its hypnotic rhythms when it chooses to be tame.

My family has learned that the beach is also an outlet for my creativity, for my inner architect to emerge as I craft sandcastles with the help of my boys. The three of us particularly love to arrive at the beach two to three hours before high tide and secure an abandoned parcel of beach near the high tide mark. Then the magic begins.

Each castle is different, but carries common themes: we always make it massive with towers three to five feet tall, with a large moat, villages, streets and bridges. Without fail, we will spend the first 20 minutes building a massive pile of sand and then we form the walls, turrets, decks, gate houses and then our very own Carcassonne starts to emerge. The boys bring water and form the outer sections while I carve and introduce the streets, walls, tunnels and plan the space.

My wife, watching from afar, sees the shift in kids at-play around us. Within 30 minutes (sometimes less), the more outgoing kids nearby start to creep over. They sense something great and even exciting is happening. They don't know what, but they see something purposeful with deep engagement, a lot of activity with buckets of water pouring as elements of the castle are form.

We include them in our work group and the water starts to pour more quickly, the villages around the castle form rapidly, and little shells and seaweed start to decorate the different parts of our beach town as more helpers arrive. My position is always along the face of the main castle, offering ideas to kids looking shy and managing the team that is forming.

Remember, I have never been a fan of child labor rules which restrict kids from finding their dreams. So, I have no problem enlisting these young and ambitious workers! As the waves start to reach a little further, the excitement grows. There are sections of the village that are wiped out and I hear chants of "We will rebuild!" or "More sand on the break walls!" Then, crash, another big wave comes in. The kids are shrieking with delight and are emboldened by the strength of our one break wall. It further ignites their passion to save the castle. Two, three even four hours pass like minutes.

At some point, I usually step away and let the momentum continue on. Older kids empower themselves and the game continues.

I get such joy from creating something from nothing, bringing a few buckets, finding some pieces of sea wood, handfuls of sand and building something that our beach community rallies behind. While the initial pieces of the castle were my ideas at the start, the ownership moves to my boys soon after and then all the others that join in make something much better and more beautiful than imagined at the beginning.

Visually, the physical beauty of our construction project is what people notice; however, the often unanticipated benefits that emerge make it possible. You see the bonds form in our micro-community as kids of all backgrounds come together to share the experience of beating the ocean, with unfettered optimism, and a sense of purpose and teamwork.

Through this project, there are many lessons that are taught. It is an opportunity to learn about the power of the waves and how to be safe in the surf, to find different aquatic species around the beach, the right water content of a properly consolidated pile of sand that allows it to better deflect a wave. The lessons are endless.

Set in the beachside with the comfortable and relaxed attitudes from parents at ease, there is always teamwork, positive feelings of sharing seen with bigger kids helping smaller ones. There is a sense of pride for the castle and surrounding village they built, a sense of purpose to support and maintain the castle and a feeling of camaraderie forms while working together.

We are all born with a willingness to come together and work together - it does not need to be learned. This inherent skill needs to be accessed, supported and harnessed for good.

This is the essence of a community-engagement project: finding an inspirational project that meets a current demand, getting people to say "I want to be part of that," and then engaging the community to seek their ideas. The development and construction then need to be supported in a way that the community can participate, learn, share, be engaged, and the space and programs that are enabled need to be stewarded. Try it the next time you go the beach, you'll have a blast!

Finding and Planning Your Inspirational Project:

If you have done your work so far, you have a sense of the footprint your charity leaves on the planet. You have identified a number of issues and problems, and are starting to put together a list of projects that you need to fund that will reduce your environmental footprint, save you money and move your organization along the continuum to becoming Sustainably Green. You have also begun empowering your staff at individual locations and they are starting to meet and think about how they can raise awareness – they will give you more projects for your green fund.

Now you need to pick one (or a handful) of projects to build into an inspirational project. You are only limited by your imagination when it comes to developing inspirational projects. The recipe for success boils down to defining the scope of the project, schedule and budget – Project Management 101 – but assembling it in a way that allows you to maximize impact and participation, as well as position it for funding and partnerships.

I have given a several examples at the end of the section, but these should be your ideas, your dreams, your vision. An inspirational project should be simple, beautiful, meaningful, and melt your heart…maybe even bring a tear to your eye. Like the pure voice of a young mellifluous singer, you just know it's good with every fiber of your being, it resonates when it's right. That song is their gift to give. This project will be one of your gifts to give to your community.

FINDING YOUR PROJECT:

Look across your organization, your community, the areas you program, operate or visit. Look for things that are problematic or that need to be rethought; look for places that are tired and due for a facelift; look for things that are broken and create an opportunity to update and breathe in new life.

Over the years, many people have been exposed to these types of projects; some examples are: cleaning up a green space, rebuilding a park area, building a community garden, and building a house for a family in-need (Habitat for Humanity built their model on this approach.) In Toronto, another local charity, Evergreen, secured an old closed industrial building in a very central location that stuck out like a sore thumb. They built a strong partnership and transformed this site into the Evergreen Brickworks and have become a leader in helping local communities transform urban spaces to green spaces. This Evergreen site is this

Lessons from Kids:

Some of my favorite stories from our projects are when things don't go as planned.

One of the first natural playgrounds that we built was at the High Park YMCA in Toronto. We closed the playground and constructed this amazing natural space – reusing the logs from a sick tree we removed, gardens, land slides – the works.

On the last day before the construction started, the kids all collected snails from their old playground and brought them inside to protect from the construction activity. As they watched the playground transform, they tended to their little shelled friends.

On opening day, the sun was shining, the local media was present, the all the parents, teachers and kids were excited. As the kids were let out to experience this beautiful new natural experience the kids were all huddled together around a bush. The adults were all confused, nobody bounded to the slide, bikes, sandbox or musical instruments. In fact, they were releasing their pet snails back into the wild and waiting for them to enjoy their new home...moving at a snail's pace.

It was a delightful reminder that nature's lessons come in all shapes and its teachers are all ages.

rallying point and a place to learn these skills. I recommend you start small to get comfortable. Start somewhere.

Step 1: Define the impact you want the project to achieve

When looking for projects, you need to make sure that they make sense as a priority for your charity so that you remain aligned with the core elements of your mission and attain internal support. In my experience, a critical ingredient is finding the educational and interpretive elements and seeking a connection to the programming you will offer to make it bigger and reach deeper. The spaces are learning and teaching tools.

Using the natural playgrounds as an example, the impact we wanted to achieve was:

Create a natural playspace in which children would continue to learn about the environment in a way that extends the classroom outside of the buildings by including natural elements such as logs (so they could watch them decompose and see bugs build homes) and trees (with leaves that bud, grow, change colors and then fall), and gardens (with seeding, weeding, loving, harvesting, and even bringing the food back into the classroom to pickle or create jam).

We wanted to connect the recently expanded learning curriculum, "Playing to Learn," to this enhanced space. We wanted the space to reflect the community in which it resides to allow multiculturalism to be incorporated into the space. We wanted the children to feel part of the designing experience so that they could learn how to design and build, and then the children will pass the sense of ownership to the next generation of kids that will use that space, child to child.

Step 2: Look at what part of the community it impacts; the more the better

The greater amount of different types of people and ages that the project can impact, the more opportunity you have to inspire people. For example, with green roofs and terraces, all segments of our communities can use them: the young and old can use them as stretching or fitness areas, school groups can access them to focus on particular learning objectives that includes alternative energy, native plant species, specific planting selection and maintenance, construction of a green roof, etc. It is accessible for persons with disabilities and safe for all to use.

For a project like the creation of natural playspaces at our childcare centres, we limit our potential users to the kids in that area that use the child care center; fortunately, there is a strong belief in communities that this type of space is a worthy investment. We extend the offer to the community to help us to build the space - at the end of the day, those playgrounds are for the families in the community, not for the YMCA or the school.

Step 3: Look at the use of space in the project; the more flexible the better.

When we look at converting spaces like green roofs and terraces, or repositioning camps, we always seek to have a variety of configurations or setups. This allows groups who use the space to add other innovative uses and to maximize participation. For example, with gardens focused on growing vegetables, we look to include movable benches and even some movable planting beds.

Step 4: Look at the variety of elements in the project; the more variety with thoughtful integration, the better.

I like to maximize the opportunity for educating and finding new and innovative ways to blend ecology with environmental technology. Sometimes at the YMCA of Greater Toronto, we pack more into the spaces than would be done in a traditional private space. There are a variety of different technologies and natural elements that provide additional opportunities for learning and interacting and there needs to be a diversity of learning experiences to ensure all ages and backgrounds find something to relate to.

In building the natural playspaces, we incorporated the traditional elements like sandboxes, slides (in the form of hill-slides that followed the terrain) and trees for shade. We then extended some of the planning to include gardens for growing vegetables and spices, indigenous structures from around the world, and a variety of interactive water elements. It is symbiotic with the space, providing the learning opportunities that allow for different activities to co-exist with thoughtful integration – the teachers love it as much as the kids!

PLANNING YOUR PROJECT

If you have progressed through the first series of steps with success, then you have developed a project that you are getting excited about. It will upgrade or evolve an aspect of your community and will allow you to bring sustainability and positive social impact through community gathering and learning in a way that will incite a groundswell of participation to bring this idea to fruition. Great job – you must feel extremely charged and ready to grab your tool belt and get started! These next steps will help you temper the project in a way that will maintain control of the process, establish expectations, facilitate participation and partnership, and get it done in a way that makes everyone involved proud.

Step 5: Define your must-haves; an important step in maintaining control.

Changing a space or creating a project that will involve engaging the community to help shape and design, you need to be extremely clear on what the "must-haves" are necessary for you run your operation, safety concerns or other limitations that may exist based on laws, agreements or shared uses. When I facilitate these types of sessions, I always tell people to divide their requirements into three groups of items:

A.   Items that you know have to happen a certain way. It is the list that defines your parameters and constraints for the project. These are the must-haves.

B.   Items around which you have flexibility and want to get external ideas and influence. These are the items that you need assistance and ideas to define. When building this list, look at your last list and make sure all of those are really "musts-haves." This is the time to challenge assumptions and to broaden your world, just not at the expense of safety or breaking laws.

C.   Other items you haven't thought of yet or don't yet know the answer. This can include items like the structural capacity of the roof, the types of plants you can plant, if a permit is needed, etc. It is also the placeholder for items that emerge that need to be relocated to item A or B above.

I can't emphasize enough how important this step is to the eventual success of your project. Before you externally engage any part of the community, you need to be very clear what you want people to affect and what you don't. This is often difficult for people to get their heads around as you are creating a tension between seeking external help and opinions, and wanting to maintain control. As well, you will notice the seemingly contradictory advice I give in items A and B.

You need to keep the must-haves close, but I encourage you to give items up for engagement. This becomes an iterative process where you need to reassess what is mission critical and what is "we have always done it that way" (but nobody remembers why). You need to manage your real risks and responsibilities appropriately.

As an example, for my first big project with the YMCA, the Central Toronto Green Roof, we decided to create a small Steering Committee that was half staff, half members from the community. We had very specific task for this group: first, to help us define in greater detail the scope of what we wanted to achieve with this project; second, define what questions we wanted answered, what feedback we were hoping to learn, and how we would access the community.

We made it clear to the Steering Committee that we were using them as sounding boards, but before we went external in a public way, we had to define our must-haves on behalf of the YMCA. Our "Parameters and Constraints" list included:

o   Minimum percentage that the roof had to be vegetated.

o   Maximum number of people.

o   Structural capacity limitations.

o   Budget constraints.

o   Use of low-maintenance materials.

o   Very safe space with open sightlines.

o   Low flammable materials to protect users

o   Universally accessible.

o   No food and drinks unless for a particular event.

o   Open from dusk to dawn, from mid-April to mid-November.

The engagement should be developed to allow the community to advise you in the areas in which you seek input - to be clear, where they can assist and clear where they cannot. When you receive their feedback, you need to review it, synthesize it, and channel it into your areas of need.

If this step isn't taken, then the parties you engage will do this step for you and will make the decisions based on their preferences and experiences. While this is often well-intended, it can lead you down a path towards broken trust when you eventually have to pull back to instill control. Don't fret over this, just make sure you work through this dynamic carefully and treat it in a principled way.

Step 6: Define your Schedule

The schedule will be affected based on seasonal limitations (e.g. weather) as well as program and building hours. Define how the space can be accessed during the day, during the week, and during different times of the year. You might want to align it with a specific holiday or activity. Costs will increase and decrease based on these choices. For example, having an electrician come in after hours or over a holiday will be more costly then during daylight hours. It might be necessary, just ensure you account for it.

Once you come back to planning a detailed schedule, make sure you add extra time for the volunteer portions to allow for additional safety training, context setting and no-shows on some projects. We have scheduled work shifts where people remain on-call for no-shows to help mitigate lost time.

Step 7: Define your Budget

When it comes to budget, I usually frame this as a two-stage process. You need to have an initial budget that meets the core aspect of the project; the minimum that you believe you have to do to get it done, and you need to share that value with your community. You can choose to design beyond this initial amount, but not build those portions until you find funding for that additional amount.

At the design phase, I set the ground rules in a way that doesn't limit creativity. For example, "We have a budget of $20,000 to renovate this space, but let's not let that limit our thinking. We can develop our larger dreams and then stage the installation based on the success of our fundraising." Each project varies, but you need to be clear what you can do, and what you are willing to do.

Step 8: Define your Engagement Strategy

How, where and when you ask for feedback will dramatically affect the success and how comprehensive the input becomes. The more avenues or channels you pursue, the greater the impact. Use meetings, set up booths, social media, email, newsletters, advertising – the more the better.

The typical strategy we follow has three stages:

Stage 1: Cast the Net & Inform

Let people know the high-level scope of the project, why you are doing it, that this will be a project that will require a lot of help from the community to help design and build. You are "advertising" to your community that this is coming and you would love for people to start thinking about your project. You are looking for volunteers to join your "Green Team" (or to start one) to help breathe life into this project; seeking sponsors for the project, and planning to build this with volunteers.

You are asking two specific questions:

a)   What are your ideas that we should include in this project? What elements, uses, or other relevant ideas should be incorporated as we start to formulate designs?

b)   How would you like to be involved?

For our Central Toronto Green Roof project, we put up signs in the lobby with cards to be filled out and returned to us. As well, we set up a blog with an email address to take feedback electronically. A lot of ideas came in, from "I want to put a tennis court or driving range on the roof" to "water fountains", "yoga studio", and "seating areas" to name a few.

Stage 2: Designing the Spaces:

The essence of this step is to have people offer more specific feedback to allow them to understand the project well enough that they can find examples in their lives or create new ideas that could potentially be included or applied to this inspirational project. It can look completely different depending on the type of project, but relies on the theme that you are seeking multiple ideas that will be considered and reviewed by the Steering Committee. Some of the time, we presented sample designs to garner comments, other times we sought help in designing.

One important trick is to not pit different camps or designs against each other; instead, try to have people offer feedback about each design. As they give feedback about what they like and what they don't like, you want to keep it positive and not competitive. It makes for a smoother transition to the final design rather than people feeling like their version didn't win.

For our large Green Roof, we decided to run a town hall meeting to launch Step 2 based on the information we retrieved in Step 1 through feedback cards, conversations and emails. We showed three different designs that included many of the ideas gathered to allow some visualization of the space, but we also offered blank slates for kids and interested designers to play with. At the town hall, we let people ask questions, give ideas and offer feedback.

We continued this theme in simple booths set up in the public lobby areas of our building, staffed with volunteers, who shared the different designs with anyone interested and requested feedback. We set them up for two weeks at different times of the day and different days of the week to encourage people on different schedules to participate. We included books that described examples of walking surfaces, plants, lighting, and layouts to further help people visualize and then offer comments. We continued to post this information on our blog and sent emails out to people who were interested. There was overwhelming feedback and ideas aplenty.

For projects that were more technical in nature, for example, a solar thermal panel system at our Scarborough YMCA location, we took a completely different strategy. Since there was not much room for help designing the solar panels, we added a solar "Eco-Fair" to the project scope that would allow for different types of participation. The community was involved in setting up information booths, speakers and activities to share in a day of learning and community-building. We included a computer display in the main lobby that explained how the solar panels on the roof energy created and reduced greenhouse gases.

When we were engaging the community to help us create a vegetable garden within a childcare playspace, we worked with a local Landscape Designer who volunteered to lead a design session with the community to do a focused design session. It was an incredibly positive experience and the ideas that emerged were brilliant, and the future sponsor ended up being part of the design session!

Stage 3: Unveiling the Design, Celebrating the Process and Mobilizing the Build:

This last step is a transition step that takes all of the hard work from the previous steps, synthesizes all of the ideas within the constraints and parameters, and yields the final concept. This is a time for celebration! The focus is to thank everyone for their participation, recognize people or companies that played a special part, and to move the process to the "community build" part of the project.

This is a great time to include media in a project, as there is something specific to show, a process to discuss, and a story to follow. If a sponsor is interested, this kind of media profile will also help to build value for their support.

EXAMPLE PROJECTS

Here are a few projects that I have worked on or am trying to put together:

Converting an Outdoor Roof-Top Amenity Space to a Green Roof Space:

Working with an urban community to design and construct a rooftop amenity space at our Central Toronto YMCA to offer a variety of spaces while keeping to a theme of outdoor fitness, ecology, environmental technology and education in a green space. Working with the same community to construct the space and then manage the space to keep it beautiful while introducing extensive programming to further educate and engage the community (see **Chapter 1: The Giving Charities Green Concept and Why This Works** for a more detailed description on the Central Green Roof.)

onverting an Unused Maintenance Terrace to a Green Terrace:

Mirroring the successes of the Central YMCA Green Roof, we engaged the community in a design process to create a deeper connection to locally grown organic food. A rooftop terrace at our Brampton YMCA underwent a participatory design process that yielded raised planting beds that are wheelchair accessible, and created a connection to the natural playground space below.

Developing Natural Playgrounds at our Child Care Centers:

At the time of the writing of this book, the YMCA of Greater Toronto had over 275 childcare centers across the Greater Toronto region and continues to grow. As part of the educational program "Playing to Learn" that the YMCA developed, playgrounds evolved to spaces that have a lot of decentralized play across different types of surfaces and spaces to facilitate diverse learning experiences. After a few iterations, the engaged approach to developing and constructing playgrounds emerged as the more effective method.

We partnered with Evergreen, a local charity that is very experienced in bringing green spaces to urban areas with an eye to education and engagement. We struck a partnership where they would facilitate an engaged design with the children, teachers, and some parents to have the kids help to design the space in a way that was specific to the existing community.

The typical elements in all of our playgrounds include hill-slides, sandboxes lined with real logs, trees for shade and planting areas. As the different school groups came together, different types of miniaturized structures were incorporated that reflected indigenous buildings from around the world to embrace the multiculturalism of our communities.

We try to align a corporate sponsor for each playground that provides a substantial donation and supplies volunteers to help build and then maintain the space in future years. These projects often form a "jump-start" approach for a new Green Team (discussed in Chapter 12 – Building Momentum with Green Teams) that extends to other parts of the building

Converting a Day Camp to an Outdoor Environmental Education and Leadership Camp:

One of the properties that the YMCA owned for over a decade was a beautiful 263 acre parcel set in the Oak Ridges Morraine, a legislatively-protected region of Ontario that forms an incredible watershed with rich biodiversity. After researching our communities and understanding the possibilities for this land, we developed a masterplan to reposition this site as a place to learn important leadership, healthy living and outdoors skills with a focus on environmental sustainability.

YMCA Cedar Glen will help to educate the children in our communities ways properly integrate a rural and protected ecology with environmental technology and development. It is becoming a place where they will discover today's solutions, and start to imagine the solutions for tomorrow.

The site has been divided into numerous areas that all intersect and blend into a perfect balance of forest management, species protection, accessibility, solar power, wind power, organic farming, commercial organic recycling, outdoor leadership training, day camping, overnight camping, international development and it even offers a small conferencing center.

Participation from corporations, foundations, and individual philanthropists, gives us the ability to keep expanding our projects and impact. Each area incorporates a significant donation, volunteerism (groups of up to 300 people at a time) and interpretive educational elements. This is a mega inspirational project that has been developed in a way to create capacity for numerous large and small corporations to get involved in something that will be a spectacular addition for schools in the region. Students and teachers can come to a space that extends their classroom for all ages.

Creating a Youth-led TV series that Focuses on Sustainability:

Working with a local TV producer to create a youth-led "news desk" where local children present stories on the type of sustainability activities that are going on in their community – both successes to be emulated, and challenges to overcome. This could yield local television content that would make up a regular television series, include corporate organizations to highlight their successes, and educate a larger community on sustainability while providing youth employment.

Developing a Local Food Waste Depot:

Working with a regional entrepreneur to locate commercial composting equipment in urban settings that would collect food waste from our food operations and create an employment training program focused on learning about running a business and working in the sustainability sector. The rich fertilizer that would be created could then be incorporated into the onsite urban garden, YMCA rooftop gardens, and then shared with the community for local plantings and gardens. By installing this type of technology in distributed locations, we would offset all of the transportation costs (and waste) and create local jobs for youth to collect the waste and distribute the fertilizer.

Collecting Batteries to Divert from Landfills:

Over the last year, one of my personal missions has been to reduce the impact of batteries on local landfills and the surrounding aquifers. Some statistics demonstrate that batteries can contribute 60 to 85% of the hazardous content within landfills, but occupy less than 1 percent by volume. Potent little buggers! Our provincial authority "Stewardship Ontario" developed a program that allows public-facing organizations to collect batteries and re-direct them to battery recycling plants that either reuse or recycle 100% of the materials contained in a battery. We have since provided battery collection bin at our large locations and are rapidly inundating our local battery recycler with a huge volume of batteries.

Action Items:

1. Find a project that will inspire your team and your community. Follow the steps in this chapter and get a project going. You have to actually go through the process to understand what will work best with your organization. This is the really, really fun part of the becoming Sustainably Green. Have fun with it.

2. Tweet your thoughts:

 @GivingGreen "inspirational project"

You never know when a moment and a few sincere words can have an impact on a life.

   - Zig Ziglar

If you don't have something nice to say, don't say anything at all.
   - Thumper the Rabbit, Bambi

Chapter 16 – Getting Connected and Communicating Your Work

Charities are notorious for doing the right thing, but not telling anyone about it. The real impact most people strive to achieve is making a difference in people's lives, not telling other people about the good work they are doing. This irony is that the better organizations are at advertising their success, the better success they have with attracting funding and creating partnerships.

While we all understand this logically, time still has to be freed up to find the success stories, identify the impacts, tally them up, and then somehow get the word out...there are never enough hours in a day, right?

Well, I must disagree. Aside from the necessity of promoting your sustainability activities, charities in general need to get better at sharing their successes and impact. I am not saying you need to start accosting people on the street and forcing information down their throats, just seek some external avenues for delivering some of the key themes that you are making a difference – and sustainability should be one of those themes.

There are tons of books written about promoting that cover this topic in detail, so I will only focus on what has worked for me and how it ties into the overall strategy. If you are struggling with this, it is time for another amazing volunteer; preferably, someone connected in the advertising world. Let them guide you through this to assist you in finding the right topics and the right outlets. As you start to get a reputation for doing cool projects, you will find that people will be contacting you and it will get easier to access media outlets.

Key Avenues to Become Connected:

Print Media (Traditional and Electronic): Newspapers, magazines, e-zines (web-magazines) and blogs (web logs or online articles that anyone with a website can write and post.) All of these media outlets have people looking for content for their articles. Once you find one or a few that cover some of the topics that you want to address, approach them and ask how you can included in an article.

In an effort to promote the YMCA of Greater Toronto, I have had people interview me, or ask for me to write an article for review. It is a fairly simple way to have your work referenced in the public domain by a third party. Once those articles start to appear, referencing those stories and articles through social media is a great "soft" approach to promoting your organization without getting overly aggressive.

Television and Radio: My experience with this segment of the media is that this is the hardest group to break into. There is great value in being profiled, but there are many challenges in seeking out the right people, being prepared and coming out looking the way you intended. Any success I have enjoyed was based on other great people arranging it.

If you are dipping your toe into this avenue to promotion your organization, save this for later in the process when you have some visually attractive projects that are really inspirational and get some help in navigating this realm. My experience is the impressions left after your 8 seconds of airtime are fleeting, and much harder to reference and search when you start to use social media to extend the soundbites.

Social Media: The new frontier over the last decade in self-promotion is social media, and it is the biggest bang for your buck. My preferred method for promoting the work we do is to seek Internet-based articles from online magazines, newspapers, or blogs, and then reference those articles using social media. At the time of writing this book, I primarily use LinkedIn and Twitter, but I am starting to use Facebook more often as well. As time marches on, new applications will likely come to market, but the strategy will remain the same.

The first decision you need to make is if you are representing your organization or yourself in the digital world. My experience relates to presenting myself as an individual because the YMCA does an amazing job as managing our organizational presence. As an individual:

- Create a profile that defines who you are and how you plan to interact in social media – your virtual persona. For example, for twitter, my profile defines me as:

"Sustainable facility design, construction and operation with insatiable hunger to be efficient while combining excellence with usefulness in the charity sector."

This should be done on an individual level and be connected to the organizational level as well.

- Build a virtual community that you want to engage in dialogue. Facebook, Twitter and other similar "friend" or "follower"-based sites allow for you to advertise and have people join your community to hear your updates. I use LinkedIn to actively seek people in the industry or sector in which I want to promote our sustainability activities. My goal was to build a group of 500 people and it has since rapidly grown to over 1,000 people "Linked In", creating a pretty good regional audience for promoting our work. You can further extend this type of promotion to different groups that are formed within LinkedIn, or form your own. This takes time to put together, but it is free.

As you are picked up in the media, or want to just make your own news, start to circulate your projects, your awards and your thoughts into this virtual community. I'll be honest, there is still a lot for me to figure out in this area, and things change quickly, so I recommend you further investigate, read and find tech-savvy volunteers to guide you through this. You are probably surrounded by people who are already doing this in their own lives.

Websites: Having a website these days is like having a shirt. Most everyone has one, some look good, some look awful, some are really old, most are clean, some pretty dirty. Some you notice and even ask about, but most are taken for granted. If you are just emerging from a coma, recently freed from a melting glacier, or returning from a desert island and don't have one for your organization – get one! For less than $20, anyone can find you and contact you. Most charitable groups are sophisticated enough that they define who they are, what they do, how to contact them and can now ask for donations online. Use a content management system like Wordpress so you can easily update it or change its look.

As part of your self-promotion, I believe that the website should be used for you to express your commitment to being Sustainably Green, advertise your Green Fund projects, highlight your partnerships, and act as a way for people to learn about what you have done and what you are doing. If you set this up efficiently, you can use this as a tool to recruit volunteers, seek partners (corporate and charity alike), seek donations, keep media and volunteers updated on the status of the project, steward donors and act as a living record of your environmental impact. You can reference your different social media outlets and link your entire virtual world together to let it work for you.

Speaking Engagements – conferences, speaker series, networking events: Getting your face in public and your organization on conference agendas is the tried and true way to build awareness with specific segments. Businesses use this to promote their products and services, and involves putting together a presentation on something that is both relevant to the conference or meeting agenda, and having a clear message to deliver.

For charities, there are a series of questions you need to answer before you take the time to pursue this approach. Below are some of the questions and how I answered them from my perspective.

Why get out there?

For the YMCA, it was decided to bring the learnings to others in the charitable sector, to actively lead in the Not-For-Profit sector for becoming Sustainably Green. Through these efforts, numerous other charities (both national and local) worked together and formed alliances to achieve our shared goals.

There was also an intention to present a solution to the commercial sector that would offer them a way to actively participate with a local charity that is making a difference in the health of children, teens and young adults; and, that these businesses could work with the YMCA through volunteerism and sharing their funds to further their philanthropic and community improvement goals. In my opinion, the day of the "check-book" relationships are a thing of the past, and the modern businesses want to have a holistic partnership with a community agency or charity where their staff can be part of that change.

Where to be?

There are so many conferences and events, that it takes time to learn what is happening, when, and to approach them. I had the benefit of doing business development for a consulting engineering firm prior to joining the YMCA, so I had a head start. I also have a strong Environmental Sustainability Advisory Council that has connections and advice.

I decided to focus on conferences that were focused on businesses and municipalities becoming more green. I also chose to be present at employment forums where youth and universities would be present. We are always seeking new and young volunteers and interns.

What do you say?

My goal with every presentation was that the viewers would remember the YMCA as a charity that is having impact on the health of our communities, is smart, current, organized, needs help to do more and is doing some really cool things in the environmental sustainability space.

Quite a few of these conferences, we were the only charity in the line-up, so I was careful to organize the presentations to incorporate business vocabulary and presented business cases and outcomes.

I assembled all of my presentations around inspirational projects and tell the story with pictures – the many diverse faces of our volunteers – learning about sustainability and improving their community as well as highlighted where key donations or funding was secured. I start off with some information about the YMCA of Greater Toronto and impact we have in our region, then I describe our journey to becoming Sustainably Green and then show a series of photos that I narrated.

How do you start?

I started by attending networking events and speaker series. I would question the speakers, the organizers and start to learn about their goals and upcoming agendas. I would plant the seed about the work that we were doing at the YMCA, and that I would be happy to share a presentation at an upcoming event. Once I got the chance, I made sure it was amazing. From there, it was just persistence and finding an opportunity. In the last couple of years, I have been speaking at four to five conferences per year, which is the most I want to incorporate into my schedule. I am now contacted regularly and turn down more than I appear at as I remain principled about my participation.

Conferences have been a successful part of our strategy for getting the word out and gaining important partnerships. We used social media to help build awareness and to extend these events out to others in our networks.

Action Items:

1. **Develop of social media profile. Build up a presence in Linked In. Build a professional profile in Facebook. Set up a Twitter account (I hope you did this already!!)**

2. **Make a list of conferences that you want to be part of. Approach conference organizers and find a session you can participate in. Even early in your journey – your willingness to be involved and share some of your early wins may be enough to garner interest.**

3. **Tweet your thoughts:**

 @givinggreen "getting connected

The more you praise and celebrate your life, the more there is in life to celebrate.
  - *Oprah Winfrey*

There are two things people want more than sex and money – recognition and praise.
  - *Mary Kay Ash*

Don't worry when you are not recognized, but strive to be worthy of recognition.
  - *Abraham Lincoln*

Chapter 17 – Celebrating Your Impact

As you picture celebration at the YMCA, I bet you have an image of everyone donning their cowboy hats, native headdresses, and police caps, with every expectation that I strap on my hard hat – be honest, you started humming that famous ditty from the Village People. Well, that's only a little bit true at the occasional holiday party. There is usually a collective groan of disbelief, then someone pulls out the trunk and the hats are passed as the frantic dancing begins.

Celebration is something we can always do more as we so rarely take time to appreciate the value of the projects or initiatives we achieve. We miss the opportunities to recognize the unanticipated implications and outcomes. We miss the chance to recognize those incredible people that makes things happen. Celebrating comes in many forms and there is no right way, as long as you take pause to acknowledge something meaningful and give yourself and others a pat on the back. Below are some of the key ones to use:

Grand-Opening Event: for inspirational projects, this is actually a necessary step to recognize the partners who worked so hard, show the sponsors how well-placed their donations were, and attract media to help share this inspirational event with the community. We often include a ribbon-cutting ceremony and have had great success including public figures to assist with the ceremony and cutting of the ribbon. Politicians bring media as well as extend the event deeper into the community.

As much as possible, we try to make the ribbon-cutting portion as short as possible, and to try to facilitate some other community activity in which people will want to participate. This has included, planting days, fitness events with famous athletes coaching local kids, and "Eco-Fairs" wher we bring in people to set up booths for information sharing coupled with children's activities.

Casual Get-together: My personal style is to invite partners or colleagues out for a celebratory drink to "cheers" the successes over snacks and a beer. There is something about food and drink (with other people serving you) that recognizes an accomplishment and marks a success. We did this after winning Canada's Top Greenest Employer award (5 times!) as well as other local awards. After the big grand-opening events that celebrate the many partners and funders, I always ensure that I take the key team members out for a more intimate and private event to personally thank them for their efforts and time.

Linked In Project or Recommendation: We work with so many volunteers and young innovative thinkers, that acknowledgement of the success in Linked In is very meaningful and useful. Taking 30 minutes to pen a project description and to include those that were involved goes a long way, as well as keeps your Linked In profile.

Old-Fashioned Card: I am a big fan of a simple card. Going old school and picking up a pen on a beautiful card is always a great way to say thank you or to acknowledge some amazing people that contributed towards an accomplishment.

When to Celebrate?

This is a personal decision, but I try to make sure we celebrate:

- Completion of a community volunteer event
- Annual Measurement of our Environmental Footprint
- Award or Recognition Event
- Speaking at a Conference
- Donation or Grant received
- Newspaper article or interview (that paints a good picture!)
- Hiring of a new staff
- End of the year to look back at our successes

- Forming a great partnership

- So much more….

Action Items:

1. After you finish the next chapter – celebrate! You've finished reading this book and should buy yourself a hot beverage and acknowledge this milestone before you start to move ahead.

2. Tweet your thoughts on when to celebrate or how to celebrate:

 **@givinggreen "celebrate"**

"Find a hobby that you love, and then find a way to make money doing it"
    -JJ Woolverton

"You must be the change you wish to see in the world"
    -Mahatma Gandhi

"Knowing is half the battle"
    -GI Joe

Chapter 18 – Tag, You're It

I recently came across a letter I wrote to myself as a teenager during my annual winter basement purge. In my junior year in high school, I went on a seven-day Outward Bound trip in the White Mountains of New England for a January winter camping experience. Winter camping was fairly new for me at the time, having gone only two or three times with my school groups the previous winter. It mixes the best with the worst of being in the outdoors: harsh cold winds, difficult trudging conditions (even with snow shoes) where you're building up a sweat that then freezes on you....and the cold nights. I'm really selling it, I know.

Oh, but once you get into the deeper woods, the wilderness you get to enjoy in its serenity and purity has no comparison. The fresh white powder covers every surface and the trees, the wildlife, and the scenery. As you step up to a view across the crest of a mountain, the only evidence of man's existence are the footprints that you just placed. Like a good workout, you work hard to get there, but the payoffs are intense beauty and a sense of deep calm.

In the midst of this experience, each of us had a 36-hour "solo" where you we're given a few acres to hunker down, some meager supplies, a task to write yourself a letter that will be mailed to you in two years, and responsibility to survive this time on your own. It was a time for introspection, self-evaluation, and an opportunity to grow by expanding your comfort zone.

My letter was simple as I recorded a poem, a map of my camp site and some words of encouragement. I looked at the first 16 years of my life and the impact I wanted to leave. In the midst of such serenity, my love for the outdoors deepened, and my passion was further invigorated to ensure that these places would remain, forever. My poem:

Winter Solo

As we trudge through the fresh-powdered snow,
Born just a few hours ago,
I see the sun creeping over the crest,
Rising, so wondrously slow,

The pine and birch are all around,
Each have something to say,
And the simple greens, browns and whites,
It's certainly nature's way,

I flick a pine bough and watch the snow fly free,
Then see a giving birch,
I gaze all around at this gorgeous scene,
It feels like MY earth!

Alex Versluis, winter 1989
Outward Bound Solo

As I re-read this letter, some 20 years later, I re-evaluated my legacy and the impact I've had and want to have. In the midst of the weather changes our planet is expressing, a better understanding of how man has altered the earth, and the legacy we leave or stole from our future generations, I worry.

Tag – you're it! I have shared my system, my thoughts, my principles, and laid it out in a way that lets you pick it up and apply it to your organization. Now what? How will you leave the planet a little bit better than you found it? As you think about the biggest highs and lows in your life, what sticks out? Your bonus? That report you wrote? Your high score on a video game? As you enter the later years of your life, will you regret a missed opportunity?

Each of us has a role to play, deep or wide. Life gives us our set of circumstances and we choose to accept them, or redefine them – turning lemons into lemonade as it were.

Now is your chance to become part of the solution. Ron Garan, former NASA shuttle astronaut describes in Planetary Collective "Overview" seeing earth from space, he reflects that it is an "indescribably beautiful planet...a living, breathing organism, but at the same time looks so fragile." Sometimes seeing yourself from a distance can help you appreciate your situation.

My hope is that you will find a way for your charity to make a change to include sustainability in everything you do. You will know you are successful when people start to ask themselves "what is the impact of this decision" and they are thinking about the environmental impact or the legacy we leave future generations. If enough people are thinking that throughout the day, each hour of the day (not just Earth Hour), each day of the year (not just on Earth Day) then we will be on the path to healing our planet for our future generations to enjoy. They will have challenges no matter what we do, but what generation hasn't been saddled with problems. Ours is to swing the pendulum back to center so that the next generations can figure out how to continue to coexist as each new generation grows.

Below is my hope for inspiration. Find yours, demand change, build your team, and inspire change. I believe that you can make a significant difference; believe in yourself.

My hope:

To ensure each child reaches their potential; is offered opportunities to explore and learn; is given hope; is supported; and, their creativity is nurtured and encouraged to bloom so they can offer their gift to give. I want them to experience the things that inspired me and have opportunities to find new ones. I want them to learn and appreciate the outdoors - hike, camp, canoe, kayak, sail, rock-climb, and see nature in its pure unadulterated form. I want my kids' great-grandkids to be able to know a vibrant and diverse forest and clean waterways, and to breathe fresh air.

ABOUT THE AUTHOR

Alex Versluis is a licensed Professional Engineer in the US and Canada as well as a Certified Energy Manager. Alex's career over the last 25 years has included designing, building, operating, fixing and expanding properties.

He studied civil engineering at McGill University in Montreal, Quebec and has worked as a consulting engineer in both Canada and the US focusing on buildings in the commercial, institutional and residential sectors. He manages the assets and facility teams for the YMCA properties in the Toronto region. He has been a small business owner as well as a senior executive in large businesses over his career.

At the YMCA of Greater Toronto, Alex is currently the Senior Vice President of Property Management and Development. In this capacity, he is responsible for the operation of over 400 properties as well as the design and construction of new YMCAs. He also leads the YMCA's environmental sustainability and resiliency program in Toronto.

Prior to joining the YMCA, Alex worked as a consulting engineer in Toronto working as a structural and building science engineer designing and overseeing building renovations, energy retrofits, and assessment with a focus on buildings that were due for renewal. During his time in the US, he also prepared geotechnical investigations, structural reviews, condition assessments and facility inspections for new construction.

He currently resides in Toronto with his wife and two teenage boys. He travels extensively and loves to write and speak with organizations on reducing their environmental footprint and energizing their communities to become more sustainably green and resilient to climate change.

Printed in the USA
CPSIA information can be obtained
at www.ICGtesting.com
JSHW062314180923
48628JS00002B/2